The Ten Laws of Happiness

To Kate Pepin with love Jon

By
Jon Mundy

Royal Fireworks Press
Unionville, New York
Toronto, Ontario

Previous Books by
Jon Mundy

Awaken To Your Own Call:
A Comprehensive Introduction to *A Course in Miracles*
Published by The Crossroad Publishing Company of New York, NY

Listening To Your Inner Guide
Published by The Crossroad Publishing Company of New York, NY

Royal Fireworks Press
First Avenue, PO Box 399
Unionville, NY 10988-0399

(914) 726-4444
Fax: (914) 726-3824
email: rfpress@frontiernet.net

Royal Fireworks Press
78 Biddeford Avenue
Downsview, Ontario
M3H 1K4 Canada

Fax: (416) 633-3010

ISBN: 0-88092-453-5

Printed in the United States of America using vegetable-based inks on acid-free, recycled paper by the Royal Fireworks Printing Company of Unionville, New York.

To My Stepdaughter and Teacher,
Sarah Holl

who is teaching me trust, honesty, tolerance,
gentleness, joy, defenselessness, generosity,
patience, faithfulness and open-mindedness.

All the things that a Teacher of God needs to learn.

I am very fortunate.

If you hold your hands over your eyes,
you will not see because you are interfering
with the laws of seeing.
If you deny love, you will not know it
because your cooperation is the law of its being.
You cannot change laws you did not make,
and the laws of happiness were created for you, not by you.

A Course In Miracles® T-9. I.11:7-9

TABLE OF CONTENTS

ACKNOWLEDGMENTS

First, I thank you for picking up this book and beginning to read it. I hope you'll read it through. The ideas we are about to explore are important, key elements in living a life in accordance with the Will of God—doing so leads to our own greatest happiness.

I wish to extend my thanks and deep appreciation to:

My wife Dolores and my stepdaughter Sarah, who are the delights of my life. With these two beautiful women I share my living, my learning and my loving.

Diane Berke, my partner in the foundation and development of Interfaith Fellowship and *On Course* magazine, who has been ever present in her love, devotion and commitment to the work we share.

Meribeth Seaman (for the past 7 years) and Julie Tyler (for the past 2 years) have worked with me in the regular composition and editing of *On Course* magazine and added their editorial suggestions and corrections.

Sara Emrie, Heather Harris and Dorothy Spellman, three good friends and members of our church, Interfaith Fellowship, in New York City, each also added their excellent editing abilities.

Suzanne Rabin, a dedicated student of *A Course In Miracles,* has added her suggestions to help keep me on course.

The members of Interfaith Fellowship, our church in New York City, who first heard many of these ideas shared in various messages on Sunday mornings; and the readers of *On Course* magazine, who first read most of these chapters as they were published in *On Course.*

Dr. Kenneth Wapnick, who has been my friend for more than twenty-four years. Ken has consistently fostered my own growth and understanding of the Course by constantly challenging me to look further and deeper. I have not always followed his advice. However, every time I took his advice, I discovered he was right. My thanks to Ken for his suggestions for changes and improvement.

Preface

A Word About The Footnotes:

A Course in Miracles was published June 22, 1976. Nearly one million copies of the first edition are in existence. The second edition contains minor corrections and revisions, and introduced the numbering of all paragraphs and sentences for easy reference. In this work all footnote citations refer to the second edition. The abbreviation "T" refers to the *Text*, "W" to the *Workbook*, "M" to the *Manual for Teachers*, "C" to the "Clarification of Terms" (found at the end of the *Manual for Teachers*), "S" to the *Song of Prayer* (a pamphlet from the same source as the Course), "P" for *Psychotherapy: Purpose, Process and Practice* (another pamphlet also from the same source as the Course). Numbers of parts, sections, subsections, chapters, lessons, questions, paragraphs, and sentences are provided as appropriate.

The ideas represented herein are my personal interpretation and understanding and are not endorsed by the copyright holder for *A Course in Miracles*® ©.

Portions from *A Course in Miracles*® ©1975 are reprinted by permission of the:
Foundation for Inner Peace, Inc.
P.O. Box 1104
Glen Ellen, CA 95442

Introduction

This is my third book on the teachings of *A Course In Miracles*. I have now been working with the Course for more than twenty-four years. The more I work with it, the more I've seen my life transformed, while seeing others' lives transformed.

In applying the principles of the Course, relationships improve, work becomes more satisfying, and everyday life becomes one of increased peace and contentment. I have come to believe that the Course is the truth, the whole truth and nothing but the truth. In no way is it lacking. In every way is it truth affirming. The Course is exciting because it works. It changes people's lives for the better.

According to the Course, fulfilling our function and achieving happiness are one and the same (W-pI. Lesson 66. 1:1-4). This book focuses on the ten characteristics of a teacher of God as described in the *Manual for Teachers* of the Course. These characteristics are: trust, honesty, tolerance, gentleness, joy, defenselessness, generosity, patience, faithfulness and open-mindedness. Living according to these principles or laws means living in accordance with our own greatest happiness.

Dr. Wapnick has noted that the Course is written in a symphonic fashion. An idea or motif is introduced and played through, then another idea is introduced and played through. Though there are different motifs, there is always one song, one message of saving grace. As we understand and apply any of the principles of the Course we automatically bring other principles into play. For example, learning to trust, to drop our judgments, to free ourselves from our anger is ultimately the same as practicing patience. Practicing patience also means being tolerant.

What is *A Course In Miracles?*

A Course In Miracles is a self-study program of spiritual psychotherapy designed to help us remember God. The memory of God is our greatest happiness. We remember God as we undo our guilt through forgiveness. Although the Course is set in a Christian context, it deals with universal spiritual themes. There are thousands of spiritual paths (M-1. 4:2); the Course represents *just one way* of reaching Heaven. The Course focuses on healing our special relationships through forgiveness. As it says in the introduction:

> *The course does not aim at teaching the meaning of love,*
> *for that is beyond what can be taught.*
> *It does aim, however, at removing the blocks*
> *to the awareness of love's presence.*
> T-Intro. 1:6-7

The Course consists of:

1. *The Text*, of some 669 pages, that contains the theory of the Course.

2. *The Workbook*, containing 365 lessons, one for each day of the year. You can spend several days on one exercise but should not try to do more than one lesson per day.

3. *The Manual for Teachers*, 92 pages, addressing some often-asked questions, such as: *How will the world end?* along with a "Clarification of Terms" found at the end of the *Manual.*

Related Material Includes:

Psychotherapy, Purpose, Process and Practice, a 25-page pamphlet that discusses practical guidelines in the application of spiritual principles to professional and personal relationships and *The Song of Prayer, Forgiveness and Healing,* a pamphlet of 20 pages that discusses the interrelationships of forgiveness, prayer and healing. These two pamphlets have now been combined in one booklet called *Supplements to the Course.*

Its Origin

The Course began in 1965 with Dr. Helen Schucman and Dr. William Thetford, both Professors of Medical Psychology at Columbia University's College of Physicians and Surgeons in New York City. Frustrated with the competitiveness and backbiting that so often characterize academia and their relationship in particular, Bill uncharacteristically turned to Helen one day and said, "There has to be another way." Just as uncharacteristically, Helen responded, "You're right—and I'll help you find it." In this ground of joining in common purpose to heal their relationship, the seeds for the Course found fertile soil and took root.

No doubt a genius with a well-trained and rigorous analytic mind, Helen was also very intuitive and sensitive to her dreams and receptive to visionary and mystical experiences. She also had a keen ability to tune in to the needs of others. Helen's chemist-metallurgist father Sigmund Cohn was half-Jewish—his mother was Lutheran. He was uninterested and uninvolved in religion. Her mother was also half-Jewish. She was for a time interested in Christian Science as well as a number of other approaches to spiritual life. Helen, though a self-described atheist, was also influenced by a Catholic nanny and a Baptist housekeeper, both of whom introduced her to their religious traditions. Helen admired priests and nuns because of their dedication to their calling. Though attracted to the Catholic Church, Helen followed no particular religious path.

In October 1965, Helen began hearing a voice which she described as "inner dictation," telling her to sit down and write. One day she called Bill to ask his advice. He suggested that it would not hurt to sit down and write and see what happened. And so began: *This is a course in miracles. Please take notes.*

The Course was published privately in 1976 by the Foundation for Inner Peace and sold by the Foundation for twenty years. In 1996 the Course was licensed to Viking/Penguin and published in a newly designed, hardcover, all-in-one edition.

The Course passed the one million mark in sales in 1992. It is now available in Spanish, Portuguese, German and Hebrew. The Chinese and Russian editions are nearing completion and it is being translated into sixteen other languages. It has probably barely begun to have its impact on the world. Thousands of study groups have sprung up around the world, and conferences on the Course are now held throughout English and Spanish-speaking countries.

The Voice of the Course

The voice in the Course is Jesus. If you believe that inspiration is something that happened, once and for all, a couple of thousand years ago or more and that is it, then you may not think this is possible. Yet the voice in the Course makes several references to his life as the historical Jesus. One may also ask, who is Jesus? Do we mean a historical figure who walked upon the earth and taught a group of followers some 2,000 years ago? Yes, but is that all? From the standpoint of the Course, to talk about Jesus is to talk about something timeless, beyond the world of birth and death. To speak of Jesus is to speak of the Christ, the Son of God, the Self that God created. To speak of the Self is also to speak of one's own true self, which always has been and will be a part of God.

My Journey to the Course

My introduction to the Course was foreshadowed by my experience as a farm boy in Missouri. There I was taken with a sense of nature mysticism that whet my appetite for religious experience. At the age of eighteen I began serving as a pastor of three rural Missouri churches (1961 - 1964). During those same years, while in college, I made frequent retreats to New Mellery Abbey, a Trappist monastery near Dubuque, Iowa. During my time in seminary (1964 - 1967), I became progressively fascinated with the study of world religions. When I was twenty-seven I spent the month of August at a Yoga ashram in Canada where, to my own surprise, I participated in a firewalking ceremony.

This firewalking experience so deepened my interest in Yoga and Hinduism that in the summer of 1971 I did a backpacking trip through India, spending time with Sai Baba, Rajneesh, and Muktananda. My last visit was with Muktananda. After several days in his ashram, I went into a cave to meditate. The cave, which was several feet underground, had no light and no sound. I sat down and said: "Am I supposed to stay here?" I had no more than asked that question when I thought I heard a loud "No!" followed by a rush of thoughts, all of which said: "Go back to New York. There you will find what you are looking for."

Back in the United States, I resumed an active career as a Methodist minister and professor at the New School for Social

Research and New York University. At NYU I met Judith Skutch, who was teaching parapsychology there. Judy was a mover and shaker in the parapsychology community in New York City in the 1970s and she frequently had friends over to meet psychics like Uri Geller or to see the latest in Kirlian photography along with other interesting developments.

In 1974 I wrote a letter that was published in the newsletter of the Association for Transpersonal Psychology. I was working on a dissertation on the relationship between psychotherapy and spirituality and my letter expressed interest in any relevant articles, books or information from the transpersonal community. In January 1975 Bill Thetford saw my letter, and he and Ken Wapnick suggested to Helen that it was a call for her to complete the scribing of *Psychotherapy: Purpose, Process and Practice.* She had scribed the first thirteen pages but never finished it.

Helen and Bill had heard me lecture in 1973 at a Spiritual Frontiers Fellowship conference in Atlanta, Georgia. We were introduced at that point, at a friend's house in Atlanta, but no mention was made, at that point, of the Course. Helen remembered our meeting and agreed that this was a call to complete the psychotherapy pamphlet, which she did in March 1975. She then called to say that she had something she thought I would find helpful.

Helen invited me to meet her, Bill and Ken at Ken's apartment in New York City the following Sunday evening. I went to this meeting not really knowing what it was about. Helen proceeded to tell me about *A Course in Miracles,* its development and its effect on those in the room. By this time I had explored many different philosophies. Most of them had left me wanting something more. Though impressed with my colleagues, I was concerned that I would again be left wanting. At the end of our meeting it was decided that Ken and I would get together for further conversations. I walked home that evening, carrying the manuscript of the psychotherapy pamphlet, feeling that probably the most important thing that had ever happened to me had just happened, but I was not sure what it was.

5

Several weeks later, in May 1975, Helen met Judy Skutch. Judy took fire with the Course; it was what she had been looking for all her life. Judy began by distributing several photocopies of the Course, making it possible for a small group of us to get an early start in studying it. Judy and her husband, Bob Skutch, together with Helen, Bill and Ken, were to start the Foundation for Inner Peace which became the publishers of the Course. The Course itself was printed and released a year later in June 1976. Bob and Judy later divorced and Judy remarried. She is now Judy Skutch Whitson.

It was not until July 1976 that I really began to take the Course seriously. Doing so was precipitated by an event that I call my "death experience." A few days after the experience, I wrote a detailed description entitled *Holy Hell,* which I read to Ken, Helen and Judy at Judy's apartment on Central Park West in New York City. Four things became clear to me from this experience: *We are not our bodies. We cannot die. We are making it up here. There is no time.*

Memories of Helen

Ken and I became friends and I sponsored a number of workshops with him as the leader (1977 - 1984). Helen, in turn, became something of a mother figure, guide, mentor, teacher and counselor in times of trouble. It seemed I was frequently in trouble, particularly in my relationships with women. Helen was always available by phone and was very supportive. She seemed to intuitively know when I was in trouble and would call to see how I was doing. She had an incredible ability to work with people in distress. At several points I felt frustrated with the Methodist church and called saying: "I've had it, I'm quitting." Helen repeatedly said she felt it important that I not quit, at least not then.

Helen was very direct and would tell me what to do in very clear terms. I was not, however, a good student and often resisted her advice. At one point she said I should let go of a relationship to which I was quite attached. I could not see how I could follow her advice and find peace. In this case, as in all others, I ultimately realized she was right.

6

One of the most remarkable things about Helen was the way she kept herself out of the spotlight when it came to the Course. Her name did not appear on early editions of the Course and was only added later to the introduction. She also avoided public lectures on the Course. The first conference on the Course was held at the Barbizon Plaza in New York City in 1978. Though she lived only a few blocks away, Helen was not there. Already the Course was being misinterpreted and Helen was disquieted by these misinterpretations. Helen died in February 1981. At her funeral, Ken gave an eloquent eulogy in which he discussed Helen's devotion to God—but at the request of Helen's husband Louis, he never mentioned *A Course In Miracles*.

The Church and the Course

My favorite PBS series of all time was *The Ascent of Man* by Jacob Bronowski. I was particularly struck by the section on *The Starry Messenger,* which discusses the life of Galileo. After Galileo invented the telescope, he was sure he would be able to convince the world that Copernicus' theory was true—that the sun and not the earth was the center of what was then the known universe. It was clear to Galileo that what he saw in the sky stood open and revealed. He thought that all he had to do was show this and everyone would listen. The results did not at all please the Church. Dr. Bronowski points out how naive Galileo was about people in authority.

Once I began to understand the Course, I was sure it would be just a matter of time before it would revolutionize the church. For fourteen years (1975 - 1989) I tried to introduce the church to the Course. During the Reagan-Bush era of the 1980s, while I was increasingly working from the Course and studying and teaching courses on the various mystical traditions and Eastern religions, mainline Protestantism was coming under increasing pressure from the fundamentalists to adopt a more conservative path. Finally, there were fundamentalists in my parish complaining that I was not preaching the *saving grace of the blood of our crucified Lord Jesus Christ.* It was true. I was not preaching sacrificial blood. I never had. Even before the Course this was one upside-down piece of thinking that I could not understand and would not advocate.

7

In June 1989 I left the Methodist church. In September 1989 Diane Berke and I started Interfaith Fellowship in New York City. We also started the publication of *On Course* magazine. Suddenly, a whole new dimension of ministry became possible. Throughout the 90's, we've been able to actively and openly talk about the Course and watch its increasing popularity and acceptance.

I still believe that the Course will revolutionize the church by turning the focus from sin, guilt and fear to love, forgiveness and peace. I now realize that this change is going to come from lay seekers and clerical seekers alike who are rediscovering the heart of Christianity as expressed in the Course. The Course may yet provide a Copernican revolution in Christianity because reality does not revolve around institutional systems of belief. It revolves around the truth.

A Course in Miracles is a philosophy of life that works for me as I know it does for hundreds of thousands of others. There are lots of ways of awakening. Still, there is but one mountain, one God—one peak experience. I may journey up the mountain from the west while you climb from the east. It makes no difference which side of the mountain we climb. We all begin from where we are. The more clearly each of us pursues our own unique path, the closer we get to the top, the more we realize that our various paths have all been leading us to the same point.

Part I

Fundamental Principles

Chapter 1

The Laws of Chaos

If you hold your hands over your eyes,
you will not see because you are interfering
with the laws of seeing.
If you deny love, you will not know it
because your cooperation is the law of its being.
You cannot change laws you did not make,
and the laws of happiness were created for you, not by you.
T-9. I.11:7-9

Are there such things as laws of happiness?
Are there certain principles we can live by
    that would make us happy?
Are these laws sure?
Would we succeed in being happy if we followed such laws?

Rules, Laws and Fundamental Principles
A law is a rule, a procedure, a description of a process by which things work. A principle is a fundamental law.
    • The laws of physics describe how things work in the physical world.
    • The laws of biology, such as the principle of capillary attraction, describe how things work in the biological world.
    • The laws of chemistry explain how things work within the chemical world. Liquids freeze and evaporate according to certain specific laws, such as water freezing at 32 degrees Fahrenheit. It is something which is very specific. Different liquids freeze and evaporate at different temperatures.
    • The laws of a state or a nation describe how things work in a given society.

The Law of Cause and Effect

If I intervened between your thoughts and their results,
I would be tampering with a basic law of cause and effect;
the most fundamental law there is.
T- 2. VII. 1:4

The most fundamental law is the law of cause and effect. One thing affects something else. I push a billiard ball across a billiard table, it hits another ball which rolls away from that one—action and reaction. The Law of Karma, as it is discussed in the East, says that what we do at one moment affects what comes back to us in another moment, in another life, or at another time. The word *karma* means *deeds* or *works*. According to the Law of Karma, one's words and deeds have an ethical consequence affecting one's lot in the future. According to the Law of Karma, our character determines our destiny. The Law of Karma says that everything one does, each separate deed of life, weighted along with every other deed, determines destiny.

It is our thoughts alone that cause us pain. Nothing external to our mind can hurt us except insofar as our thinking makes it so. There is no cause beyond ourselves that can bring us oppression. There is nothing that has the power to make us sick or sorrowful unless we give it the power to dominate our mind (W- 190, 5:1-5).

A miracle is a higher order cause and effect that reverses physical laws. Principle number 9 from *The Fifty Miracles Principles* says:

Miracles are a kind of exchange.
Like all expressions of love,
which are always miraculous in the true sense,
the exchange reverses the physical laws.
They bring more love both to the giver *and* the receiver.
T-1. I. 9:1

Jesus in the Gospels repeats this law as: *as you sow, so do you reap*. In street terminology we say, *what goes around, comes around.*

Cause and effect are mutually dependent. The existence of one determines the existence of the other. Belief in an effect establishes cause. Without effect, cause cannot be.

- A cause produces a result, a consequence.
- A cause is something that is responsible for a result.
- An effect is something that is brought about by a cause.

Thus, the thought of separation is the cause of our dream of suffering and death.

Everything that is happening at any given moment is the result of the choices we are making in the moment. The way we see the world is the determiner of the world we see. If we see it as damned, we are damned. When we see holiness and hope we are joined with the Will of God and set free (T-21. In. 2:2&3).

Some Course Basics—An Appeal to Reason

We can talk about three different kinds of minds in the Course.

Wrong-minded thinking which operates according to the dictates of the ego.

Right-minded thinking which operates in accordance with the guidance of the Holy Spirit.

Dr. Kenneth Wapnick has also coined the term **decision-maker** to refer to that part of the mind which chooses to follow either the dictates of the ego or the guidance of the Holy Spirit.

Within this world of illusion, we are *free* to engage in wrong-minded thinking and be separated or split off from the Mind of God. This split we call the ego. The ego can be defined as that which defines, interprets, projects, judges and analyzes. The ego is always making up the world and we are always making up the world. The ego is then a wrong-minded attempt to perceive ourselves as we *wish* to be rather than as we are (T-3. IV. 2:3). Just as we are free to dream we made a wrong choice, we *appear* to have a choice to return to right-mindedness. There is no split or separated mind in Heaven. In Heaven choice among different options is impossible. However, within the split mind, choosing between the ego and the Holy Spirit is meaningful.

12

The Holy Spirit living by the laws of God is completely reasonable. The ego living by the laws of chaos is completely unreasonable. In fact, the ego is insane. This does not make it bad but it does make it unreal. The principles or laws that operate in the world of the ego are the laws of chaos. Chaotic laws work according to the principles of sin, guilt, fear, denial and projection. The laws of God are the principles that include purification, forgiveness, healing and freedom. In the following pages I may refer to the laws of the ego and the laws of chaos interchangeably. I may also refer to the laws of happiness and the laws of God interchangeably.

This whole world and everything within it got started from a *tiny, mad idea at which the Son of God remembered not to laugh* (T-27. VIII. 6:2). This world came into existence (insofar as it exists) with the *insane* notion that it was actually possible to be separated from God.

This *is* an insane world,
and do not underestimate the extent of its insanity.
T-14. I. 2:6

There is no area of our perception that insanity has not touched. Every aspect of this world is insane. We live with relationships that have varying degrees of insanity in them. We abide by governments that have certain insane precepts or actions. We live by religions with unreasonable and insane precepts. For example, if someone is granted an annulment by the Catholic church then the marriage never existed, even though the couple may have been married for 30 years and had six children.

On the whole our perception is completely upside-down and backwards. It never occurs to us when we look in a mirror that we are seeing everything backward unless perhaps we are wearing a name tag where it may then become obvious that something is amiss. Still we accept the reality of our image as backward. What we see with physical eyes is also true on a mental level. Psychologically speaking, we see everything upside down and backward, but it does not occur to us that we do unless something happens which shows us something is amiss. The way we have set things up in this *seeming* world, its problems can never be solved because the mind trying to solve them is split—insane. Being insane, the logic of the split mind leads to nothing.

> Insane ideas have no real relationships,
>   for that is why they are insane.
>   T- 13. X. 2:1

We should not underestimate how insane the world is. Dictators have come to power, found justification for their insanity and persuaded millions of others that their insanity made perfect sense. We are all insane, insofar as we believe in the reality of the ego. We are all insane, insofar as we live in the dream world of the past rather than choosing the Holy Spirit's correction right now. Thus, the Course asks us to question whether it is *really sane to perceive what was as now*. If all we see when we look at our brother or sister is the past, then we are unable to see reality as it is now. (T-13. VI. 1:6&7).

The ego has an incredible hold, one we do not shake off readily in good part because we don't want to. We don't even know that we can. You can't change your mind if you don't know you have one. On the wall in my office are a number of tools which we used on the farm back during the 1940s and '50s. One is a small powerful metal device with a spring around a cylinder that you placed around the soft middle section of a bull's nose. There was a rope attached to this little device that you could use to lead the bull around and the bull would then go with you wherever you wanted. Even as a small child I could lead our bull around without fear. If the bull resisted and pulled back, the spring would tighten on the soft part of the bull's nose; so to let up on the pressure the bull had to move forward and follow you. The ego has a similar hold on us and tenaciously leads us around by our nose as though we had no choice in the matter.

The purpose of the Course is to help us *at removing the blocks to the awareness of love's presence* (T-In. 1:7). Our blocks are all the things which cause us to feel alone and afraid. We remove the blocks by looking at them for what they are (or, better, what they are not), and discovering that we do not need them, we let them go. Thus it is that we can shift from insane thinking, to following the *reasonable* guide of the Holy Spirit.

14

We undo the negative, to become aware of our right minds. We undo the negative by becoming aware of that which has blocked our way. It is not necessary, however, to understand all the complexities of the ego nor the laws of chaos under which it lives. The ego is a false premise, and there is no need to go mucking about in an unending examination of the false. This was one of the problems of Freud. He understood the ego very well. He even outlined a host of ego defense mechanisms. Freud, however, did not see a way out. From the Freudian perspective we are trapped by the ego and there is no freedom from its autocracy.

The Authority Problem

The basic problem we all have is the authority problem. The ego will never ask God for help or seek to live by the laws of happiness. By definition it cannot. It is clear with my daughter, Sarah, as it is with all children, that the basic problem is one of authority. Whose will will win—hers or her mother's and mine? Every child believes that their parents are out to steal their individuality from them. Sarah wants to do things the way she wants to do them. If she does not get her way she is unhappy. She is a typical child. We are all typical children in our relationship with God. What we say to God is: "Thank you very much, God. I would really rather do it myself." Being a good parent, God does not condemn us for our waywardness but patiently waits for us to come around. Eventually, we will do everything according to His laws. Ultimately we have no other choice but to choose for our own greater happiness. We could even make that choice right now.

Monism or Dualism—Unity or Chaos?

The Course differs from traditional Christianity in that the Course presents us with a monistic perspective. Traditional Christianity presents us with a dualistic (split) perspective; there is a Heaven—but there is also a devil, and guilt, and fear and the threat of eternal punishment in an everlasting hell. Once we have a split (insane) mind we have a choice between good and evil, Heaven and hell. The Son of God appears to be living in a divided state—never quite satisfied with things the way they are. We try to live our lives with a little bit of Heaven and a little bit of hell. We cannot, however, have both, and to choose to live with a divided mind is to choose to be unhappy.

15

Heaven, according to the Course, is a state of mind in which there is no dissension, discord or division. There is only one God and there is only one way of being happy. It is to live in accordance with the laws of God. However, we accept the insane notion that it is actually possible to think a thought outside of the Mind of God. We thus live within the fictitious dream world of the ego. This world is a dream, a fantasy, an illusion, delusion or hallucination. Sometimes it may also seem like a nightmare. According to the Course, all our time is spent dreaming. Our sleeping and our waking dreams have different forms and that is all (T-18. II. 5:12&13).

The real world is a reflection of Heaven. Heaven is all that is real. God and His Kingdom are wholly true; the illusory (insane) world is wholly false. It is not bad. It does not need to be destroyed and we need not try to escape from it. Destruction is the way of the ego. Defenselessness is the way of the Holy Spirit. Our task is to awaken to our reality and that is all.

You can think of our predicament as one we see in the cartoons where our cartoon character has a devil sitting on one shoulder whispering into one ear and an angel on the other shoulder offering some very different advice. The split mind tries to listen to both voices. A whole mind listens only to that voice which speaks for its own greatest happiness—the Voice for God. Actually, there is no devil (or ego), though living within the world of the ego it is hard to believe in the non-reality of the ego or the devil.

Looking at Our Dark Lessons
In order to be free, we must be willing to look at our dark lessons. We look at our dark lessons not to affirm their reality, but to discover their non-reality. Illusions cannot hurt us. However, as long as we keep our dark lessons buried in the unconscious, we will fear their potential power over us. Who among us has dreams that contain no fears? How deep does the darkness descend? We have each been *tripped up* by our own selfishness. Benjamin Franklin, who strove very hard for perfection, was dismayed that the one virtue he simply could not master was humility. Think you are spiritually advanced, and you might find ego presenting itself in the form of specialness and again you're lost.

16

It is impossible to be happy and find freedom from our illusions unless we look at our illusions. No one gives up an addiction until they are willing to admit (at least to themselves) that they are addicted. Who among us can therefore give up our specialness unless we are willing to look at it? The Course is a course in purification. We let go of that which we do not need and accept the Holy Spirit's Atonement. We cannot escape from illusions unless we are willing to look at them. Not looking at them, we keep them buried in the unconscious where they can continue to wreak havoc in our lives.

No one can escape from illusions unless he looks at them,
for not looking is the way they are protected.
T-11. V. 1:1

The ego lives by the *unreasonable* laws of chaos that simply make one miserable. We are truly happy when we live by the laws of God or the laws of happiness.

The 'laws' of chaos can be brought to light,
though never understood.
Chaotic laws are hardly meaningful,
and therefore out of reason's sphere.
Yet they appear to be an obstacle to reason and to truth.
Let us, then, look upon them calmly, that we may look beyond them,
understanding what they are, not what they would maintain.
T-23. II. 1:1-4

1. Truth is different for everyone. In a world of separation, truth *is* different for everyone but there is no separation in God's Kingdom. Truths of this world are not eternal. To say that truth is different for everyone is to say that there is a hierarchy of illusions. There is no hierarchy among miracles. *One is not bigger or harder than another* (T-1.I.1:1). There is also no hierarchy among illusions. One illusion is as good as another. It is still an illusion. Truth is One. There is no gradation.

2. Each of us must sin. Therefore we deserve our unhappiness (T-23. II. 4:1). It is easy to see sin in our brothers and sisters. We may also see ourselves as miserable sinners. We see sin and we believe in punishment as payment for sin. This is an insane

17

idea. What is needed is not punishment but correction. For eleven years I worked as a Professor of Philosophy and Religion for Mercy College, teaching in the New York State prison system. As I would approach the gates at Sing Sing to teach my classes I noticed that the sign outside of the prison said it was a correctional institution. But the ego does not know how to correct, only punish.

Sin calls for punishment as error for correction,
and the belief that punishment is correction is clearly insane.
T-19. II. 1:6

3. God also believes that we are sinful and God hates sin—therefore God hates us and is out to get us. The image of God in the Bible is a split one. On the one hand he loves us; on the other he is willing to destroy us for our waywardness. He destroys Sodom and Gomorrah, or the Philistines, or sends plagues upon the Egyptians and finally drowns all the Egyptian soldiers because he is not happy with them. This is not a God you want to upset. This is a jealous God with an ego. His ego can be hurt and when it is he attacks. God is thus a god of vengeance and not forgiveness. This is an insane notion. Reason holds that God is wholly love and nothing else and His Will for us is perfect happiness and nothing else. If you are afraid of God how can you possibly turn to him for help? If we cannot turn to God for help salvation is impossible.

4. You can have what you want by taking it. This is a good example of upside-down, backward thinking. This is the law of Genghis Khan and the criminal's justification for his actions. We live in a 'go for it' society: get it; make it yours; might makes right; possession is 9/10ths of the law; we win at someone else's loss, etc. Enemies do not share that which they value. So it goes in the backward thinking of this world. Here are some examples of the upside-down, backward, and insane thinking of this world.

In This World:
We believe we can be happy by making others feel guilty.
• are justified in withholding our forgiveness.
• can find peace of mind if we become wealthy or famous.
• can stop murder by murdering murderers.
These are all insane ideas.

18

5. There is a substitute for love. If I am justified in my righteous indignation then my vengeance is after all only what is called for. A friend called, mad as hell. She was going to call another friend and tell her exactly what she thought of her in no uncertain terms. I thought this was not a good idea but she insisted. Her intended victim was, after all, worthy of her wrath and she was only going to give her intended victim the bad karma she had chosen for herself. I told her it was her own thinking that was causing her pain but she did not believe me. Working in a backward and regressive manner, the laws of the ego lead to our own greater misery. It is the ego's fundamental doctrine that what we do to others we escape (T-15. VII. 4:2). The ego laws lead us to misery. The laws of God lead to greater happiness.

These *are* the laws on which your "sanity" appears to rest.
These *are* the principles which make the ground
beneath your feet seem solid.
And it *is* here you look for meaning.
These are the laws you made for your salvation.
They hold in place the substitute for Heaven which you prefer.
T- 23. II.13: 1-4&8

It Is Insane to Live in a World of Guilt

A woman in a workshop told us a story of how as a young Catholic girl she was required to go to her first confession but she could not think of anything to confess, so she made up a lie. She told the priest that she had told a lie. She made up a lie that she had lied. She then felt so guilty for telling a lie to a priest that she never was able to go back to church again.

As long as we value guilt, we will not look within for guidance. Yet, guilt is always totally insane and has no reason (T- 13. X. 6:2).
Who among us is free of all lying?
Who among us does not engage in denial and repression?
Who among us has not been jealous or envious?
Who among us has not projected our own irresponsibility onto others?
Who among us does not carry around a load of guilt, conscious or unconscious, that weighs upon us?

19

Children do all these things. Adult children do all these things. Insofar as we do any of these things we hold on to our unhappy way of thinking. What is needed is a wise choice, a more reasonable, happy decision.

The Regressive Laws of the Ego

The ego's laws are strict, and breaches are severely punished.
Therefore give no obedience to its laws,
for they are laws of punishment.
And those who follow them believe that they are guilty,
and so they must condemn.
T-13. IX. 1:4-6

The laws of cause and effect work in the world of the ego, as they do in the world of Spirit. The ego's laws bring into play principles of retribution, retaliation, reprisal and revenge. The ego's laws are laws of jealousy, envy, anger, aggression and attack. It is the law of *an eye for an eye and a tooth for a tooth.* According to ego laws, if you insult me or hit me, I in turn can insult or hit you back. It is automatic. I don't even think about what my response is going to be. You hit me (cause) so I hit you (effect). Your hitting me is the cause of my hitting you. The problem is that, living according to ego laws, we never get what we really want. We just think we do, for we momentarily feel as if we've unloaded our guilt. But in fact we've reinforced it. Laws of the ego are *regressive,* not *progressive.* Rather than leading to greater happiness they lead to greater unhappiness.

Chapter 2

The Laws of Happiness

A law is a rule of conduct established by some authority. The laws of happiness were created for us—not by us (T-9. I. 11:9). Therefore they must have been created by some *higher* authority. Therefore, they are *higher laws* which transcend social, institutional, and even physical laws like those of space and time. Ego laws are deprecating. Higher laws multiply or add to, resulting in abundance. Ego laws are regressive; therefore they subtract and lead to loss and scarcity. The higher mind thinks according to the laws Spirit obeys and therefore honors only the laws of God (T-5. I. 1:6).

Just as the physical world follows the laws of physics, so the Holy Spirit follows the laws of God's universe of which it is a part (T-5. III. 2:5) and the ego follows the laws of the particular and specific world of which it is a part. While we are living according to the laws of the ego, the Holy Spirit cannot help us because we are not living according to God's laws. All is not lost, however, for the ego is doomed to failure. One day we will respond and start living according to God's laws. The sooner we respond the happier we will be. We could even start today. Principle number 19 of *The Fifty Miracle Principles* reads:

Miracles make minds one in God.
They depend on cooperation because the Sonship
is the sum of all that God created.
Miracles therefore reflect the laws of eternity, not of time.
T-1. I. 19

The laws of eternity are not bound by the laws of time and space. A miracle, then, often appears to be "miraculous" because it does not depend upon physical laws of space and time. Healing does not have to be something that happens over time. It could happen in any instant in which peace comes into the mind. Laws of eternity are *reflections* of higher laws. Higher laws lead to our greater happiness.

21

They speed up the process by moving things into another dimension, no longer bound by the same confines that existed in the past.

Accepting Responsibility: How Spiritual Laws Work

It is easy to dodge our responsibility, but we cannot dodge
the consequences of dodging our responsibilities.
Josiah Stamp

The more responsibility I accept for what I perceive, the less I see myself as a victim and the more freedom I have to change things. To talk about responsibility means to talk about doing the right thing, the proper thing. Changing our thinking changes everything. Austrian psychologist Viktor Frankl, in his book *Man's Search for Meaning*, describes his life inside Nazi concentration camps and his discovery of *his last remaining freedom*, namely, the freedom of being able to choose his response to even the most degrading of circumstances. Accepting responsibility sometimes means *swallowing a bitter pill*. Sometimes it means I have to work extra hard or at night or in the cold, etc. However, swallowing that pill, or working extra hard also enables me to have more control of my life.

We begin to change when we accept responsibility for absolutely everything we do and think. Jean-Paul Sartre, French philosopher and author of *Being and Nothingness*, once said: "I am responsible for everything. I bear the whole responsibility without being able, whatever I do, to tear myself away from this responsibility for an instant."

In every instant of every day, every one of us is responsible for everything that seems to be happening to us. Sometimes when you're traveling a back road you might come upon a sign which reads, "Travel at your own risk." The sign is there to help absolve the highway department of anything that might happen on a road that is unfinished or in disrepair. In the journey of life we each travel at our own risk. We are the responsible party. Our friends, our neighbors, our parents, the community in which we live, our schools, our teachers, our relatives cannot make our decisions for us. We are ourselves responsible. We do the traveling and we incur the risks.

We give strength to that to which we bear witness. As Jesus expresses it in the Course, "A good teacher clarifies his own ideas and strengthens them by teaching them" (T-4. I 1:1). The more we take responsibility for the circumstances of our lives, the more capable we are of responding at yet a deeper level. None of us knows how strong we can be until we take responsibility for our mental and physical health, for our relationships, for our economics, for our well-being in the *seeming* world—for absolutely everything.

Someone once said: The man who blames others for his problems hasn't begun his education. The man who blames himself has begun his education. And, the man who blames no one has finished his education. Our only real hope of happiness is to realize that we are not victims and whatever seems to happen to us is something we asked for.

> I am responsible for what I see.
> I choose the feeling I experience, and I decide
> upon the goal I would achieve.
> And everything that seems to happen to me
> I ask for, and receive as I have asked.
> T-21. II. 2:3-5

Reversing the Laws of the Ego:
The Move into Hyperdrive

Accepting responsibility means taking things to a higher level, but what do we mean by a higher level? In the movie *Star Wars*, our hero, Hans Solo, and his companions are able to get away from Darth Vader and the evil empire by putting their space craft, the Millennium Falcon, into hyperdrive, thus moving entirely into another dimension. In a similar way when we move from the laws of the ego to the laws of God we take things into a wholly new, safe dimension.

When I was nineteen years old, my high school sweetheart, with whom I was very much in love, ran off and married another man. She needed to get away from home and I wanted to complete college before we got married. But she was in a hurry and took off when an opportunity presented itself. I was completely crushed by this experience. We spent the afternoon together the day she ran away. There was nothing I could do to dissuade her from what she was about to do. That night I did not sleep. It was the worst night of my life. This was my first love and I had lost her. We had never made love as we were going to wait till we were married. Now my head was filled with visions of her making love with another man. I did not know how I could possibly look at this situation and see peace. I did not understand how this was for my own greater happiness. Now, with hindsight, I'm able to look at this situation and place the event in its proper perspective, and take it to a higher level where there is no pain.

When we take any place of *stuckness* and apply a higher set of laws, not of the ego, but those of God, we are able to get peaceful results. By moving into hyperdrive and letting the Holy Spirit handle the situation instead of relying on the ego, we allow a miracle to take place. This is why miracles go beyond physical laws. They are laws of a higher celestial order.

Happiness is the gift we receive through living according to a higher order of laws. In order to do this we must *experience a reversal in our thinking* so that we do not automatically react according to lower order laws of the ego.

> Perception's laws must be reversed,
> because they *are* reversals of the laws of truth.
> The laws of truth forever will be true,
> and cannot be reversed; yet can be seen as upside down.
> And this must be corrected where the illusion of reversal lies.
> T-26. VII. 5:2-4

> Your holiness reverses all the laws of the world.
> It is beyond every restriction of time, space,
> distance and limits of any kind.
> W-38. 1:1-2

In the Gospel of Matthew, Jesus says that he has not come to destroy the law but to fulfill it (5:17). To fulfill the law Jesus takes it

24

to a higher level, far beyond the automatic response of the ego. In the Gospels of Matthew and Mark, Jesus says that he has come to bring us a *new commandment*. We no longer have to live according to the ego's laws. We do not have to respond in Pavlovian fashion to every negative thing that seems to come our way.

How the Reversal Works:
- If someone insults or affronts me,
  I do not have to respond from the position of my ego.
  I do not have to respond by being insulted.
  I could respond in love.
- If I am delayed in traffic,
  I do not have to become impatient.
  In fact, this is a perfect time to practice patience.
- If I witness some form of behavior I do not agree with,
  I do not have to be judgmental just because it is a form
  of behavior I would not engage in myself.
- I can apply higher laws and be tolerant and open-minded
  and get a much better response (effect) than I will
  by feeding into perceived negative material.

Forgiveness is the key to reversing the laws of the ego. Forgiveness undoes sin by demonstrating that sin has no effect. One day Dolores reprimanded Sarah for something, I've forgotten what and it does not matter, but there was a reprimand and I backed up Dolores. Sarah, disappointed that I had backed up mother, turned on me, reached into her arsenal of defenses and pulled out the biggest gun she could find and fired back: "I hate you." She then turned and ran upstairs. Sarah is actually pretty good at forgetting and forgiving and in about twenty seconds she returned and said: "I'm sorry." To which I responded: "It's okay honey, nothing happened." What I meant was that nothing had happened. I did not get upset because an eleven-year-old child has said: "I hate you." I know that she loves me. This was just the biggest gun she could pull from her arsenal at that moment. If I had gotten upset and come back with: "You can't talk to me that way," we would have had a problem. Not perceiving an attack (a cause) there was also no effect. Within minutes the two of us were sitting on the couch, she leaning up against me while we each read our books. If we can truly demonstrate that the peace of God and our loving relationship with Him are completely unaffected by what others do, sin cannot be a cause and thus cannot exist. This point is crucial in understanding the Course.

How Do We Interpret What We See?

Of all the laws and rules there is one which is basic to every religion of this world. It is the simple Golden Rule, that says, *the way we treat other people is the way we treat ourselves.* Giving and receiving are one. The Golden Rule is not just a good idea; it is a principle, a rule, an axiom, a truism, a law exemplified in nature. It is a description of a process by which things work, like: *as you forgive so are you forgiven.*

*Do not condemn your brother
until you have walked a mile in his moccasins.*
Native American

*Do naught to others
which if done to thee would cause thee pain.*
Hinduism

Hurt not others with that which pains thyself.
Buddhism

What you don't want done to yourself don't do to others.
Confucianism

*Regard your neighbor's gain as your own gain
and regard your neighbor's loss as your own loss.*
Taoism

*In happiness and suffering, in joy and grief,
we should regard all creatures as we regard our own self,
and should therefore refrain from inflicting upon others such injury
as would appear undesirable to us if inflicted upon ourselves.*
Jainism

Do not do unto others all that which is not well for oneself.
Zoroastrianism

26

What is hateful to yourself, don't do to your fellow man.
Judaism

*Whatsoever ye would that men should do to you,
do ye even so to them.*
Christianity

Treat others as thou would be treated thyself.
Sikhism

*No one of you is a believer until he desires for his brother
what he desires for himself.*
Islam

*Lay not on any soul a load which ye would not wish
to be laid upon you and desire not for anyone
the things you would not desire for yourself.*
Baha'i

*When you meet anyone,
remember it is a holy encounter.
As you see him you will see yourself.
As you treat him you will treat yourself.
As you think of him you will think of yourself.
Never forget this, for in him you will find yourself or lose yourself.*
T-8. III. 4:1-5

And finally as a wrong-minded misinterpretation of the rule:

I do unto others what they do unto me, only worse.
Jimmy Hoffa

The Golden Rule is the law for proper conduct in every situation. We cannot behave properly unless we perceive rightly. (T-1. III. 6:4&5). What do we want to give? What would we like to receive? Our response, our interpretation, determine everything. Interpretation is the meaning we assign to another's behavior. How we see someone else determines our response. See evil and we will hate it. See love and we will love it. What we see is what we get. This is why the world needs our forgiveness. We must give it in order to receive it. A miracle is the way things are supposed to work. A miracle is perfectly natural. Love is perfectly natural. It is the way to behave. It is not just a good idea. It is the law by which things work when they are working right. Since we are all equal members of one family we need to look out from the perception of our own holiness to the holiness of others (T-1. III. 6:6).

From the perspective of our own holiness, we see the holiness of others and thus find holiness within ourselves. We cannot recognize that which is holy unless we see ourselves as holy. We cannot look upon that which seems hateful and not be full of hate. It's all a matter of how we wish to think. As Jesus expresses it in the Gospels: *As a man thinketh in his heart so is he.*

Living by the laws of the ego means living in a tyrannical state. We obey its laws because we think we have to. Those who suffer from an addiction to alcohol or drugs or food do not feel they have any choice in their decision making. Of course they do have a choice and can experience immense freedom when they exercise the choice not to give in to the dictates of the ego. One line from lesson 354 from the *Workbook* reads: "My oneness with the Christ establishes me as Your Son, beyond the reach of time, and wholly free of every law but Yours." (W-pII. 354. 1:1) Once we no longer have to live according to the laws of the ego and can live according to a higher order of laws—laws we take joy in obeying—the result is our own inevitable happiness.

What Do You Do About Being Crazy?
We stay dumb, stupid and unhappily insane as long as we think there is no escape; as long as we believe this world and all its accouterments, the paraphernalia, the fluff and bobbles, and the soap opera of everyday life are valuable to us; as long as we are caught in illusion and unwilling to look at the truth—the insanity remains. Yet, reason, pure, beautiful reason—thinking with our right minds—can lead us out of chaos and into Heaven.

Mullah Nasurdin was down on his hands and knees looking for something in front of his house. His neighbor came by and said, *"Mullah, what are you looking for?"* He said, *"I'm looking for my keys."* So his neighbor got down on the ground and began looking with him. After an hour of searching the neighbor finally said: *"Mullah, where did you lose your keys?"* *"I lost them in the house,"* said Mullah. *"But there is more light out here."* We cannot find what we are looking for when we are looking in the wrong place. We look in every direction except where we need to look because we are afraid of our darkness. We are afraid of our own insanity; therefore we cannot know God.

Nothing of this world can make us happy. There is no amount of money, or sex, or drugs, or fame and fortune that can bring us happiness. With anything that this world has to offer, the result is always that we are left wanting. Even if we get something we have been longing for, we soon find that it does not bring us peace. So the first step is to stop looking where the answer is not.

To be happy we have to give up our addiction to the insane soap opera of our everyday lives. Fortunately, there is a way out. We need to turn over our craziness. We don't need to *do* anything. We simply need to *undo* and *let go* of the tangled webs we have spun for ourselves. We need only give up our neurosis and our psychosis. On our own, we do not know the way. We need help and the Holy Spirit is willing to help us. Twelve step programs work because of the willingness of the participants to say, *"I don't know what to do. Help me!"*

The Good News Is That:
No matter how insane we may be, no matter how often we choose to live by the laws of chaos, God's Will for us is perfect happiness and nothing can keep us from it. As the Course expresses it:

> Your wildest misperceptions, your weird imaginings,
> your blackest nightmares all mean nothing.
> T-13. XI. 7:2

They all mean nothing, for once we are awake, once we relinquish the past and allow for the present, there is no more guilt, no more insanity, no more separation from God and no more unhappiness.

A Course in Miracles is both hard and easy. It seems hard because of the complexity that *seems* to exist within the world of the ego. Yet the Course is simple, for
- once we decide to let it all go;
- once we decide that we cannot decide on our own;
- once we become receptive to help, help can come.

If we really knew how beautiful Heaven was, if we knew the peace that is possible, we would not want to hold on to a single shred of guilt, no matter how attractive it might seem. Peace is possible. Sanity is possible. It is possible to know the peace of God. It is possible to be happy. We just need *a little willingness* to turn it over. All we have to do is to be willing to give up our insanity. Of ourselves we know nothing—but with Him we can know everything.

The Laws of Happiness
The Course describes ten characteristics of a teacher of God. These ten characteristics describe various *attributes, traits, principles or laws* by which things happen. They describe processes by which things work. They are laws of happiness. According to the laws of happiness, as we are trusting, honest, tolerant, gentle, joyful, defenseless, generous, patient, faithful and open-minded, so are we at peace—so are we happy.

There are basic laws related to **trust.**
Trust is the most basic of all laws. All the other characteristics of God's teachers are dependent upon trust. Trust is broken down into several stages of development and we will look at each stage. The main question is: in whom do I place my trust? Do I rely on the ego and its laws which only get me into misery, or can I go for a higher order of laws and trust that following higher laws will get me what I really want?

There are basic laws related to **honesty.**
This topic is so important, it's the longest chapter in this book. The ego never looks on what it does with perfect honesty (T-11. In. 2:6). Hiding is a trap. Sharing is liberation. Hiding traps us in guilt. To hide is to wallow in guilt and become increasingly lost. We do not realize the enormous waste of energy we expend in

30

denying truth (T-9. I. 11:1). Honesty is crucial to our happiness. As we acknowledge the truth, we find the truth coming our way.

There are basic laws related to **tolerance.**

Jesus in the Gospels says: *As we judge so are we judged.* It's the old law of cause and effect. As we measure it out to another, so is it measured out to us. Who among us really wants to be judge of our brother? Who among us has the right to judge another? None of us knows how far a brother or sister is along the way. Very simply, God's teachers do not judge (T-4. III. 1:1).

There are basic laws related to **gentleness.**

God's teachers are incapable of harm and are wholly gentle (M-4. IV. 2:1). As we are kind and gentle, so do we find kindness and gentleness coming our way.

There are basic laws related to **joy.**

The law of joy is more one of effect than cause. Joy is an inevitable result of gentleness and the experience of freedom from fear. Joy is a consequence of following the laws of God. We can be joyful only insofar as we are ourselves trusting, honest, tolerant, gentle beings.

There are basic laws related to **defenselessness.**

Workbook lesson 153 says, "In defenselessness our safety lies." Defenselessness is a good example of the reversal process. Rather than bringing into play the ego's principles of retribution, retaliation, reprisal and revenge, defenselessness is deferential and disarming. It is peacemaking. Defenselessness, not defensiveness, brings us joy.

There are basic laws related to **generosity**.

Here the law of cause and effect is clearly seen: *As we give so do we receive.* It is silly to think that we can hold anything unto ourselves. It is especially obvious that whatever love we give away is forever ours. Generosity is a blessing we give ourselves.

There are basic laws related to **patience.**

Here again, the law of cause and effect is clearly operative. Practicing patience, we become patient people. *Only infinite patience brings immediate effects* (T-5. VI. 12:1). Those who are certain of the outcome can afford to wait (M-4. VIII. 1:1). Practicing patience, I also practice tolerance, open-mindedness and defenselessness.

There are basic laws related to **faithfulness.**
Faithfulness is the teacher of God's trust in the Word of God to set all things right. Faithfulness, like honesty, also means consistency. Faithfulness in practicing the principles of the Course brings rewards. Hanging in there, remaining true, remaining constant and steadfast gets us where we want to be.

There are basic laws related to **open-mindedness.**
Open-mindedness comes with freedom from judgment. Just as judgment is a means of closing the mind, so open-mindedness opens us to the full experience of God.

Switching into hyperdrive, teaching and practicing the laws of God—the laws of happiness—lead us to happiness and peace. This is real peace, real joy. This is what we want.

Chapter 3

Cleaning House

To make real progress we are eventually going to have to look at the last thing the ego ever wants us to. The last thing the ego wishes us to realize is that we are afraid of it (T-11. V. 8:1). We may be willing to examine lots of other things, but the one thing we are least likely to look at is that which we are afraid of. We think that something awful would happen to us if we did. Yet Jesus asks us not to be afraid to look within. The ego tells us all is black with guilt within and bids us not to look (T-13. IX. 8:1). If the ego admits the existence of God, then it must deny its own reality. Therefore the ego will not allow for the awareness of God. However, the denial of God is also the denial of our own true Identity.

Dumping Garbage

If you are going to build a house you must first muck about in the mud in order to build a firm foundation. First we dishevel the room to clean it. Three mornings a week, I begin the day by dumping garbage. The garbage truck comes on Tuesday and Friday mornings, and the recycling truck on Wednesday, so I begin these three days by cleaning out everything we do not want or need. Dumping garbage is a good exercise. Most of us begin the day by taking a shower and cleaning our bodies, making our beds and establishing an order for the day. It's good to begin the day by doing some cleaning. In order to set the mind in order, it's sometimes necessary to begin by setting our environment in order. The mind is fresh and clear and we know what we need to do to bring more order into our lives.

We might think of spiritual growth as a pruning down or cutting away of the unessential in order to make room for that which is essential. The dictionary defines garbage as *that which is worthless or nonsensical matter*. In computer science it means *meaningless or unwanted information.* The Course is helping us understand what is meaningless, or illusory, and therefore unessential.

Making the Darkness Open

Principle number 7 from *The Fifty Miracles Principles* says that *Miracles are everyone's right, but purification is necessary first* (T-1. I. 7:1). This is the only one of the 50 Miracle Principles that says in specific terms what needs to happen before there can be a miracle. Nothing is going to happen till we demonstrate a willingness to accept responsibility and change and nothing is going to change until we demonstrate a willingness to look at all the garbage we collected along the way, all the stuff we do not need. The Course is trying to help us sort out the false from the true in order to be done with the false and be left only with the true.

> The Holy Spirit asks of you but this:
> bring to Him every secret you have locked away from Him.
> Open every door to Him,
> and bid Him enter the darkness and lighten it away.
> At your request He enters gladly.
> He brings the light to darkness
> if you make the darkness open to Him.
> T- 14. VII. 6:1-4

A student once called asking the question: *Are we supposed to bring the darkness to the light or the light to the darkness?* We are to bring the darkness to the light and not the light to the darkness because we do not know what the light is. If we knew the light we would be the light. We know more about the dark than we do the light as we have been mucking about in the dark for a long time. It should therefore not be surprising that we know more of what's going on with the ego than we do with the Holy Spirit.

Like Adam in the Bushes

Jesus brings the light to us. We have to thus make the darkness open to Him. Like Adam in the bushes, we're still hiding from God—or at least trying to. Of course, it's impossible to hide from God but we try by denying God.

34

We are afraid to look at the dark, yet it is only by taking responsibility and looking at our dark side that we have any opportunity for advancement. We are afraid that looking at why we feel guilty would just be too awful. The last thing any of us wants to look at is our own irresponsibility, so we keep defending ourselves to ourselves. Yet when we are afraid of anything we acknowledge its power to hurt us (T-2. II. 1:4).

I have heard Gloria Wapnick say that when she and Ken would travel around the country giving lectures people would occasionally comment on how beautiful and light and full of love the Course is. Gloria would wonder if they were reading the same Course as she. Our experience with the Course may at first glance be beautiful and pleasing. However, unlearning the ego's specialness is a process that, by its nature, is grievous to the ego. No one likes to confront the painful, distressing aspects of one's personality. Dr. Carl Jung describes how in therapy one day a 45-year-old patient suddenly blurted out: "But I could never admit that I wasted the last 25 years of my life!" Many people stop working with the Course at exactly the point when it could be really helpful. We stop when the Course asks us to look deeper and be more honest. We stop because we resist change.

Before we can ascend to the Self, we must first be willing to look at the self (ego); and we don't want to because it looks too unpleasant. It looks too much like work. We'll probably have to change and that is the last thing we want to do. We have to go down the ladder with a willingness to look at our own darkness in order to find another ladder that reaches further up than the one we came down. Therefore we must be willing to look into the dark. Recognizing and accepting some of the seemingly bad things—not judging them—just letting them be and seeing that they were in fact a part of the illusion of our ego, we can move a long way toward an awareness of who we really are as a child of God. The Course thus says that all our *dark lessons must be brought willingly to truth, and joyously laid down by hands open to receive, not closed to take* (T-14. XI. 4:6).

You who are steadfastly devoted to misery
must first recognize that you are miserable and not happy.
T-14. II. 1:2

35

There is a saying that misery loves company. The ego thinks misery is happiness (T-14. II. 1:3), having no idea what happiness really is. We tend to associate happiness with whatever makes us comfortable; vegetating on the couch and watching television, eating good food, looking good, having fame, fortune and money in the bank. There is nothing wrong with vegetating on the couch, looking and feeling good, eating good food and having money in the bank. Yet, each of these things may also be used a distraction. A *dis-traction* is something that takes us off track.

One day I stopped dead in my tracks when I read the following sentence from Workbook lesson 133:

> When you let your mind be drawn to bodily concerns,
> to things you buy, to eminence as valued by the world,
> you ask for sorrow, not for happiness.
> W-pI. 133. 2:2

On another occasion I was meditating, and really "letting go"—just opening up in willingness to look and all of a sudden I saw something I did not entirely want to see. Meditation is "supposed" to bring us peace of mind, not distress us, but at that moment I took a good look at my selfish, greedy, lustful, hungry, uncaring, unsharing side—the great *wanting creature.* I took a look at how sensual, arrogant, and sometimes gluttonous I had been, how resistant I have always been to authority, especially the church. It wasn't fun. But I had to be honest. How often have I *let my mind be drawn* to bodily concerns—to things I buy, to eminences as valued by the world? How often has the result left me feeling like I was still missing out on something?

I read with interest James Redfield's *The Tenth Insight* in which he talks about a metaphysical principle related to what he calls one's life plan. Are we following the Holy Spirit's plan in our lives or are we following our own plan? The Course provides us with a plan and asks us simply that we be willing to turn things over to the Holy Spirit because he knows the smooth way, the easy course.

36

Denial of the Truth: Repression and Concealment

The first and most fundamental defense mechanism that keeps threatening thoughts and memories from consciousness is denial and the ego exerts utmost vigilance about what it lets into awareness (T-4.V.1:3). In Goethe's *Faust*, the devil identifies himself as *the spirit of denial.* One day, as Linus and Charlie Brown were walking along chatting, Linus says: "I don't like to face problems head on. I think the best way to solve problems is to avoid them. In fact, this is a distinct philosophy of mine. No problem is so big or so complicated that it cannot be run away from."

Having buried a great deal of guilt we need to look at the depth of our guilt in order to be free of it. We become free of the devil by calling the devil by name. But, no one wants to look at the dark places in which they have been hiding.

> The escape from darkness involves two stages:
> First, the recognition that darkness cannot hide.
> This step usually entails fear.
> T-1.IV. 1:1&2

Repression was one of Freud's earliest discoveries. Freud noted that, even with considerable probing, his patients were still unable to recall traumatic or psychologically damaging childhood events. Traumatic memories, he said, were concealed from awareness by strong forces. Freud and the Course are in agreement about our propensity for denial. Each of us has denied and repressed more than we are capable of knowing. Actually, denial has no power in itself, but we give it power and if we use it to deny reality, reality is gone for us (T-7. VII 1:5&6).

Freud said that we all spend a considerable amount of energy trying to conceal as much as we can from each other, and even from ourselves. The anxiety generated in this process of concealment, Freud felt, is the basis of neuroses and psychoses. This is the same thing as Dr. Brad Blanton is saying in his book *Radical Honesty:* that the source of all our mental illness is our hiding.

- We start gaining weight and pretend we are not.
- We spend too much money and try to ignore the debts.

• We may notice symptomatic expressions of denial in our physical or emotional functioning, such as sleepiness, disturbed memory, emotional indifference and apathy. I once knew a woman who slept all day long every Saturday, convinced that she needed a full day of sleep to overcome a week of work.

No one likes to be confronted with what they perceive as unpleasant aspects of their personality. We don't even like to be told that we *might* be mistaken. Who likes to be confronted with selfishness or extravagance? Confront an alcoholic or drug addict about his addiction and you will probably run into considerable denial. Yet no real change or freedom is possible until we admit that things have become unmanageable.

Denying or ignoring matters that really need our attention keeps us from awareness of our true identity. We thus find excuses for inappropriate behavior. "I couldn't help it." "I didn't know." "It wasn't my responsibility." When someone does something inhuman they might excuse themselves by saying: "After all, I'm only human."

Our biggest problem is not the defenses and excuses we give to other people; it is the defense we offer ourselves. Other people can handle our defenses better than we can; the last one we are willing to take our guilt to is ourselves, so we do dumb, stupid things and then we say to ourselves, "Well I know I did that, but after all I'm dumb and stupid."

When we use denial we put ourselves in an unhappy position. If something is upsetting us and we are not fulfilling our destinies, we can ignore the whole thing by *pretending* we just cannot find our true destiny. This does not make the problem go away. Denial might be thought of as *selective forgetting* or *selective remembering.* We remember what we want, or what we can deal with, and forget the rest.

Pseudo Problems
One of the ways we typically deny the reality of God and the truth of our identity is by becoming obsessed with lesser issues, what Ken Wapnick calls "pseudo-problems."

By becoming involved with tangential issues,
it [the ego] hopes to hide the real question and keep it out of mind.
The ego's characteristic busyness
with nonessentials is for precisely that purpose.
Preoccupations with problems set up to be incapable of solution
are favorite ego devices for impeding learning progress.
T- 4. V. 6:4-6

We can hide and pretend, we can bury our heads in ostrich-like fashion, we can busy ourselves with lesser things, but eventually we are going to have to look at the truth. The problem with denial is that the repressed material is really not forgotten and continues to gnaw away at our psyche. Like a cavity in a bad tooth, it slowly works its way toward the nerve. Eventually, whatever we are hiding must be acknowledged. As Jesus said in the Bible: "There is nothing hidden that shall not be revealed."

Examples of Denial

Gail Sheehy, in *Pathfinders*, tells the story of a depressed woman faced with a mid-life crisis who consistently refused to acknowledge her unhappy marriage. She eventually got out of her depression only by admitting to herself and others that the situation was, in fact, not okay and that she needed help.

A man intent upon becoming wealthy may choose to ignore the deleterious effects his pursuit is having on his family. We may completely forget to pay a bill for some extravagance. We may forget to do a job that seems noxious to us. We may forget an appointment with the dentist. We easily *overlook* things that cause us discomfort. Psychologists have given names to some of the major forms of denial.

1. **Reaction Formation,** or the replacement of an anxiety producing impulse by its opposite.

The purpose of reaction formation is to make a person unaware of the original source of distress. Someone afraid of their own impulse toward homosexuality may thus express hatred of homosexuals. Crusaders who *protest too much* against what they see as reprehensible behavior are often repressing their own feelings or impulses by projecting them onto others. Those bent on exposing sins and waging *holy wars* against *evildoers* conveniently overlook the fact that their actions go against the teachings of Jesus. Generally the stronger the impulse toward socially unacceptable behavior, the stronger the defense against it.

2. Displacement as Denial

Here an impulse or feeling is redirected to a different, less threatening person than the one to whom it is really directed.

> You are accustomed to the notion
> that the mind can see the source of pain where it is not.
> The doubtful service of such displacement
> is to hide the real source of guilt,
> and keep from your awareness the full perception that it is insane.
> Displacement always is maintained
> by the illusion that the source of guilt,
> from which attention is diverted,
> must be true; and must be fearful,
> or you would not have displaced the guilt
> onto what you believe to be less fearful.
> T- 3. X. 1:1-4

Children are often the unfortunate recipients of displaced anger. Carried to an extreme, displacement becomes a phobic reaction, a profound and irrational fear of certain things such as cats or snakes or spiders. Behind every form of denial is the guilt of separation and fear of retaliation from God. In fact, *allegiance to the denial of God is the ego's religion* (T-10. V. 3:1).

The Course is asking us to be honest. Very honest. It is asking us to look at ourselves. We are very good at not looking at ourselves. We do not let ourselves be who we could be because we are in denial. The good news is that once we've taken a good long look at ourselves, like the Prodigal Son, and we're really clear that the answer lies not in some of the things we chose in the past, like fame, money, pleasure, and power, we can then choose the right response and start climbing back up the ladder toward God.

When we see our mind going in a certain direction, ask: *do I really want to go there?* In order to experience a turnaround we must admit at some point that we've been wrong. Instead of engaging in denial we now correct the wrong choice instead of swearing it was right and defending it.

Ken Wapnick has been implacable in teaching me this important lesson. He perpetually holds up a mirror that enables me to see a side of myself I don't always want to look at. I have frequently gone to Ken and asked him for his comments and criticism. Whenever Ken has had a criticism of me, it's always struck me that I should try to look carefully at what he has said and see if I can learn from it. I have not been really good at this. I was not good at it with Helen Schucman either. I often resisted her advice too. When I'm really honest I discover that I allowed my mind to be drawn away—to bodily concerns, to things I buy, to eminences as valued by the world and, insofar as I have, this has kept me from my own happiness.

Denial of Illusions: Correction

The Course speaks of a positive use of denial, namely the denial of illusions. When we notice that our mind is being drawn toward some "distraction," that is precisely the time to use the denial of illusion. Whenever we notice fear coming up, say, in conversation with a friend, it is a good time to refuse to be a part of this fearful dreaming, by not giving energy to the fear. This is admittedly not easy, because the ego has a great need to judge and is quick to jump to judgement. What we need then is *a little willingness* to let what is true be true. While all that is called for is *a little willingness* we might not forget that the Voice that asks for *a little willingness* is also the Voice that calls the entire history of the physical universe "a tiny tick of time." Jesus' perspective is a little different than our own. The ego has a tremendous investment in hating and blaming others and it requires a great deal of hard work, vigilance and discipline—to have the little willingness that is called for in order to let "what is true be true" (T-26.VII. 10:1).

The proper use of denial:
• hides nothing.
• prevents anything not of God from affecting us.
• brings all error into the light.
• corrects error automatically.

41

True denial is a powerful protective device. We should deny any belief that error can hurt us in any way. This kind of denial is not a concealment but a correction. Our right mind depends on it.

Denial of error is a strong defense of truth,
but denial of truth results in miscreation, the projections of the ego.
In the service of the right mind the denial of error frees the mind,
and re-establishes the freedom of the will.
When the will is really free it cannot miscreate,
because it recognizes only truth.
T-2. II. 2:2-7

The more we take responsibility, the stronger we get and the better we feel. Spiritual growth occurs as we take a good look at ourselves—at our guilt and fear. Our fears show us the blocks we have to an awareness of love's presence. Reestablishing freedom of the will means the acceptance of responsibility. It is a conscious decision to make the right choice in each and every instance.

As we move into love and forgiveness, the need for defenses disappears. Holding to the central core of who we really are—not as a fearful ego, but as a peaceful spirit who is capable of seeing—facilitates our own greatest happiness. Thus, when a situation has been dedicated wholly to truth, peace is certain (T-19. I.1:1).

Purification is of God alone, and therefore for you.
Rather than seek to prepare yourself for Him, try to think thus:
I who am host to God am worthy of Him.
He Who established His dwelling place in me created it as
He would have it be.
It is not needful that I make it ready for Him,
but only that I do not interfere with His plan to restore to me my
own awareness of my readiness, which is eternal.
I need add nothing to His plan.
But to receive it, I must be willing not to substitute my
own in place of it.
T-18. IV. 5: 7-13.

42

Chapter 4

Always, Only
Never and Nothing

The Holy Spirit will help you reinterpret
everything that you perceive as fearful
and teach you that only what is loving is true.
T-4. IV. 1:3

I particularly enjoy passages in the Course that use words like *all, only, always, wholly, completely, forever, eternally, everything, everyone, nothing,* and *never.* Words like *always, only never* and *no* are categorically clear. They give a definite direction. There is nothing ambiguous about them.

Always, means *all ways* — forever and eternal.
Never comes from *not* and *ever* meaning *not ever.*

Examples include:

Attack is *always* made upon a stranger.
T-3. III.7:3

The *only* aspect of time that is eternal is now.
T-5. III.6:5

. . . *only* infinite patience produces immediate effects.
T-5. VI. 12:1

(Note: Italics added for emphasis.)

Acknowledging the truth is *never* about evaluating. It is a matter of *knowing* what is true, not trying to *figure out* what is true. Ken Wapnick says the question is not "why can't I hear the voice of the Holy Spirit" but, "why don't I do what He asks me to do so I can hear his voice even better."

43

Truth can *only* be recognized and need *only* be recognized (T-7. IV.1:1). If we are figuring, we are still figuring. To figure is to plan or to decide. Lesson 135 from the Course Workbook says: "A healed mind does not plan. It carries out the plans that it receives from a wisdom that is not its own" (W-pI. 135. 11:1). The Course is not about evaluating, interpreting, projecting, judging or trying to figure things out. Here are a few instances of the 1,852 times that the word *only* is used in the Course.

• First some *onlys* regarding the mind.

Only the mind is: real, responsible for seeing,
in need of healing, capable of illumination.

Only the mind can: be sick, value, decide, create, be shared.

Since the Holy Spirit is in your mind
your mind can also *only* believe what is true.
T-6. II.10:3

Only minds communicate.
T-7.V.2:1

Only one-mindedness can be without confusion.
T-3.IV.3:3

• Here are a few examples using *only* and *ego.*

. . . *only* the fearful can be egoistic.
T-5. IV.1:3

. . . *only* the ego can experience guilt.
T- 4. IV. 5:5

. . . *only* the ego can be disheartened.
T-4. IV.7:4

• And here are a couple regarding *only* and *spirit.*

Your reality is *only* spirit.
T-1.III.5:5

Reality belongs *only* to spirit,
and the miracle acknowledges *only* truth.
T-I. IV.2:4

• Here are a few *onlys* regarding *love.*

Only perfect love exists.
T-1.VI.5:3

... the *only* possible whole state is that of love.
T-5.In.2:2

Teach *only* love, for that is what you are.
T-6.I.13:2

• And a few on *peace.*

Only peace can be extended.
T-7.VI.12:3

The *only* way to have peace is to teach peace.
T-6.III.4:3

• Here are just a few of the 652 times the Course uses the
word *never.*

... holiness ... can be hidden but *never* lost.
T-1. I. 31:3

A miracle is *never* lost.
T-1.I. 44:1

False concepts are *never* real except to ourselves.
T-1.VIII. 3:7

The mind *never* sleeps.
T-2.VI. 9:5

Good teachers *never* terrorize their students.
T-3.I.4:4

45

Knowledge *never* involves comparison.
T-4.II.11:12

It (the ego) *never* dies; it was merely *never* born.
T-5.IV. 2:3

Never forget that the ego is not sane.
T-5.V.3:8

(Note: Italics added for emphasis.)

Some Course Basics
Mind is all that there is.
Everything happens on the level of mind.
It's *never* a matter of what is going on outside.
It is *never* a matter of form.
The form is just a reflection of things
—it is never the thing itself.
All thinking produces form on some level. (T-2. VI. 9:14)

Nothing happens on the level of form which is not first in the mind.

One day Sarah said something sarcastic to her mom. Then she said it was an accident, it just slipped out. It was not something she had thought. It is impossible that we could say something that we had not thought. *Everything* we perceive is a witness to the thought system we want to be true for us (T-11. VI. 18:3).

What Are We Thinking?
Living on the outside means living in an artificial world, a world of the ego's own making. As the ego dreams or makes up the world, there is then *nothing* outside of the way something is seen. For good or for ill *everything* is determined by the way we see things. Everyone identifies himself with his thought system and every thought system is centered on what one believes one is.

If the center of the thought system is true,
only truth extends from it. But if a lie is at its center,
only deception extends from it.
T-6.V(B).1:10

For this reason all false systems of belief will eventually fail. The totalitarian Soviet distortion of communism fell apart on its own because it wasn't true. In 1991 I became aware of what seemed to be *A Course in Miracles* cult formed around a charismatic leader. I was concerned about this possible misinterpretation of the Course and called Ken Wapnick to express my concerns. Ken's response was to quote a piece of scripture which said: "If this be of God there is nothing you can do to stop it and if it is not of God it will come to naught."

The question is: *What do we want to send out from our mind?* How do we see things happening for ourselves in the present and in the future? As we give so do we receive. Our thoughts are either of our right mind or our wrong mind.

- Right-minded thinking is *wholly* true.
- Wrong-minded thinking is *wholly* false.
- What is wrong-minded thinking?
    Wrong-mindedness consists of the belief in:
- *sin,* the idea that we can be separate from God.
- *guilt,* the experience of being separate from God.
- *fear,* the emotion that follows guilt.

- *Sin* is our relationship to the past.
- *Guilt* is our experience in the present.
- *Fear* is our anticipation about the future.

Right-minded thinking shifts our mind from wrong-minded ego thinking (the belief in sin, guilt and fear) to seeing things the way the Holy Spirit does, which is to see everything with love.

One-mindedness

Seeing everything with love returns us to one-mindedness. Rev. Sara Emrie, one of our associate ministers at Interfaith in New York City, keeps saying, *"Why don't we just say things the way they really are. We are One."* It's not just a nice idea. It is the way things are.

- One-mindedness is the Mind of God or Christ.
- One-mindedness is a unified Mind.
- One-mindedness exists only in Heaven.

If I experience one-mindedness I experience Heaven, even if I'm in a body on planet Earth.

Heaven is here. There is *nowhere else.*
Heaven is now. There is *no other time.*
M-24.6:4-7 (Italics added for emphasis.)

Have you ever been so fully in the moment that there was no where else?

• One-mindedness exists only on the level of knowledge.
It is a matter of knowing, not a matter of trying to figure something out.

More Course Basics
Having established that mind is all that there is, let's take another step and recognize that:
All thinking is either projected or extended.
• To project means to throw or to hurl away.
• Projection is our attempt to try to blame someone else
for the separation we ourselves feel.
• Projection reinforces guilt by displacing it.
• Projection is *always* a means of justifying attack.

Only the Holy Spirit is conflict free.
Only the Holy Spirit is capable of right-minded thinking.

Anger is *never* justified.
T-30.VI.1:1

Jesus doesn't say anger is *sometimes* justified. The ego would love it if he did. If Jesus said anger was *sometimes* justified then we could debate about which times anger was justified and which times it was not, which would call into play our evaluating minds.

• Extension is the ongoing process of creation
— spirit extending itself.
• *All* loving thoughts are extended

48

and *only* loving thoughts are true.
- Loving thoughts create the real world.
- *All* other thoughts are illusion—fantasy.
  They contain no reality. They are not eternal.

A Little Logic

If *only loving thoughts are true* then all other thoughts must be false. This is an incredible idea. Any idea I have about you which is not loving is not true. If I see Sarah as anything other than the perfect innocent child of God that she is, I'm misperceiving her. What I see then has nothing to do with God and His Kingdom. It has nothing to do with what is true about the You that You really are. In truth You are the Son of God. Therefore there is no attack which I can level against another which is not a misperception.

Only when we accept complete responsibility for the ego's existence can we lay aside all anger and attack (T-7.VIII.5:4).

There is *no* attack which can ever be justified.
- *All* attack is meaningless.
- *All* attack is indefensible.
- *All* attack is unjust and *only* appreciation is an appropriate response to a brother (T-12. I.5:8).

One day I hailed a taxi in New York City. The ride was miserable. The cabby honked the instant each light changed in an instantaneous Pavlovian response. Though he was never at the front of the line, I felt as though he would have honked even if he had been the first in line. He attempted to run a red light and thus got us stuck in the middle of 42nd Street and 9th Avenue, blocking traffic and causing gridlock. He asked me four times what my destination was and when we finally got there he buzzed right past it. When we finally stopped I found myself wanting to tell him how much I had not appreciated his driving. Then I remembered the line from the Course which says, *"only* appreciation is an appropriate response to a brother." At that moment I did not feel appreciation of any sort; nevertheless, Jesus said it and therefore it must be true so I decided to hold my tongue.

Later that day I made a visit to a men's room in a bookstore. There was water all over the floor and when I left I sought out the management and informed them of the problem. This was not perceived as an attack and was not meant as one. The same could not have been said about the way I felt about the cabby. If I had said anything to the cabby I am sure my tone of voice would have come across as an attack.

We have to decide in each and every instance if our attempt to help correct a problem is an attack or a sincere attempt to be helpful. *All* attempts to try and "fix" other people come from our failure to understand that, if we are all one, and we *are* all one, finding fault with anyone is also *always* a form of finding fault with ourselves.

> Think about the way God sees things.
> God thinks *only* loving thoughts.
> Is there anything that God cannot do?
> Yes. God cannot think an unloving thought.

That is what the ego tries to do. It *tries* to think a thought in isolation. It tries to make the unreal real. Even God cannot make the unreal real. To try to think a thought outside of the mind of God is insane thinking. The Course says *that into eternity there crept a tiny mad idea at which the Son of God remembered not to laugh* (T-27. VIII.6:2). The tiny mad idea is the idea of separation which first entered into the mind of the Son of God. It is the idea we still hold today. When this tiny mad idea first appeared, we should have laughed at it. That is not, however, what we did. We took it seriously and thus began all our problems. Though the tiny mad idea entertains the idea of separation—it is not true. *Nothing* ever happened. We never left Heaven. We are only dreaming that we did.

God offers us His love unconditionally. The perception of God as a father or mother who loves us without condition is a good way to think of God. The only separation we think can ever occur is in our minds. Sin, guilt and fear exist *only* in our minds. It is impossible for sin, guilt and fear to be a part of God's mind. What is of God's mind is *wholly* true. What is not of God's mind is *wholly* false.

50

Lesson No. 74 from the Workbook says that:
There is no will but God's
and this idea is *wholly true.*
Nothing exists outside of the Mind of God.
You are a part of the Mind of God.
It is the only part of you or me that is wholly true.
Everything else is a fantasy.
Everything else is an illusion.

Fearful Thoughts Are an Appeal for Help

Any thought about our own lack of wholeness comes from fear. It is part of the illusion. We should accept only loving thoughts in others and we should regard everything else as a call for help. Whenever anyone seems to behave in an unwelcome manner, it is because they are afraid and in pain. We have all been in pain. We have all been in fear. We know what it is about. *No one* likes to be projected onto. We cannot help others by projecting onto them. We help others *only* by ourselves *being* a demonstration of the characteristics of a teacher of God: *trustworthy, honest, tolerant, gentle, joyous, defenseless, generous, patience, faithful* and *open-minded.* It is in this way that we offer our love. We nurture peace in others *only* as we nurture peace within ourselves.

It will be given you to see your brother's worth
when all you want for him is peace.
And what you want for him you will receive.
T- 20.V.3:6

As we give *so* do we receive. Whatever *seems to be* happening is always a reflection of our inner thinking.

No fearful thoughts are true. All loving thoughts are true.

Nothing real can be threatened.
Nothing unreal exists.
Herein lies the peace of God.
- ACIM Introduction

51

Part II

The Ten Laws of Happiness: Characteristics of a Teacher of God

Chapter 5

The Law of Trust

You have very little trust in me as yet,
but it will increase as you turn more and more often to me
instead of to your ego for guidance.
The results will convince you increasingly that this choice is
the only sane one you can make.
No one who learns from experience that one choice brings
peace and joy while another brings chaos and disaster needs
additional convincing.
T- 4. VI. 3:1-3

There Are Two Teachers in Our Mind

It is up to us to decide which teacher we are going to listen to. We experience the world from the perspective of our teacher. Who shall we choose to learn from, the ego or the Holy Spirit?

When it comes time to trust:

• The ego tells us not to trust in God. It says that if we do we will be destroyed.

• The ego therefore tells us to place our trust in the ego.

• Deep down inside we know, however, that we cannot trust the ego (T-4. I. 8:2). This leaves us in a state of anxiety.

Trusting the Ego

When the ego is our teacher the world is seen as a place of sin, suffering and sadness. When we put our trust in the laws of the ego, defenses of all sorts are necessary. A host of ego defenses are available for us, not only a whole battery of psychological defenses like denial and projection but many literal defenses; our special relationships, money, insurance policies, guns, guard dogs, electronic surveillance, etc. Such is the way of the world. This is not to say that we should not have insurance nor lock our doors at night. It's just that these things contain no *real* security. Inner peace does not depend upon the external. Real security comes in a deep trust in God.

Jesus placed His trust in God no matter what. Trusting in the love within us, resting in the arms of God is the only true safety.

When the Holy Spirit is our teacher we find a forgiving world. When the Holy Spirit is our teacher we can no longer be victimized by the world. The more we trust in God and rely upon the Holy Spirit's guidance, the more clearly we understand how petty are the ways of the ego. How ridiculous it is to think that one can get one's way by, as an example, throwing a temper tantrum. The 1995 bombing in Oklahoma City was not only tragic in the eyes of the world, it was also ridiculous. It is ridiculous to think that we can get what we want by being destructive. Peace is possible but we cannot find peace by making hell.

> You who have tried to learn what you do not want
> should take heart, for although the curriculum you set
> yourself is depressing indeed,
> it is merely ridiculous if you look at it.
> T-12. V. 8:1

The curriculum of the ego is ridiculous, indecorous and depressing. Copping an attitude, getting angry or blowing up a building will not get us what we want. If you hold a gun to the side of someone's head, you may get compliance but it does not make you right. Attack only increases our guilt and leaves us with a growing sense of anxiety.

- Who wants to live an artificial life?
- Who among us would seek to live the life of a soap opera?
- Who would play out a tragedy?

Many people live in nightmarish and soap operatic lives. Teachers of God are not interested in soap operas. They are no longer dependent on their egos, but look to Spirit for guidance. More and more they choose to trust in the guidance of the Holy Spirit.

> Who would attempt to fly
> with the tiny wings of a sparrow
> when the mighty power of an eagle has been given him?

> And who would place his faith in the shabby offerings of the ego
> when the gifts of God are laid before him?
>
> M-4. I.2:2-3

Who would? You and I would, insofar as we do not trust in God. Yet, it is possible to go ahead and live our lives based on the guidance of the Holy Spirit rather than our shabby egos. Doing so gives us a wholly new and joyful outlook on life. Once we let God's strength be that on which we depend, everything changes.

Trusting God—Trusting Others—Trusting Ourselves

We cannot talk about trusting God without talking about trusting our fellow man. If we are all one, we must also trust each other. There is an old saying: "The individual who trusts others will make fewer mistakes than he who distrusts them." It is better to be taken advantage of than to be the one who takes the advantage, or as Will Rogers expressed it: "I would rather be the man who bought the Brooklyn Bridge than the man who sold it."

Every good partnership is based on trust. Every good marriage is based on trust. As we develop and deepen our relationship with the Holy Spirit, as we increasingly come to trust the Holy Spirit in every way, we come to understand that a partnership with the Holy Spirit is going to lead us home again and enable us to find what we are really looking for.

Trust is something we develop. That which is developmental takes time. There is no time as such in Heaven, but we do experience time in this world. Learning to trust in the laws of happiness takes time. As we apply these various principles and see their results in our lives we can increasingly depend upon them and therefore bring them into practice.

As we cannot trust the ego, we must place our trust in a deeper source. We should be grateful for the failure of the ego in this regard for it brings us back to God again.

Six Stages in the Development of Trust

The Course describes six stages in the development of trust. These six stages are not finely delineated. Though the Course describes them as first, second, and third, etc., there is a lot of overlapping.

1. The Period of Undoing

When the Atonement works within us, it is a process of undoing. Purification is a process of removing the junk that covers the core of wholeness. It's not a matter of doing but a matter of *undoing* that enables us to hear the Voice for God. Just as it is in *not eating* that enables us to lose weight, so it is in not making error that we come to the truth.

Undoing *need not be painful* but it usually is (M-4. I. (A). 3:2). It is usually painful because we feel things are being taken away from us. In a literal, worldly sense, we might lose money, friends, property or self-esteem of the ego variety. Actually, the only thing we lose is that which contains no real value. We are only losing an illusion. Losing an illusion makes us wiser than finding a truth.

It may be difficult to see how a mortgage foreclosure, a bankruptcy, a divorce, the death of a loved one or facing one's own death can be helpful. Spiritually speaking, however, it invariably is helpful and with the benefit of hindsight we can see that the loss was a necessary part of our development.

> When the heart weeps for what it has lost,
> the soul laughs for what it has found.
> Sufi Saying

In 1989 I went through a dark night of the soul involving the loss of a country inn and restaurant that I had purchased after the sale of my home the previous year. With the benefit of hindsight I now see that I went into this endeavor wearing a number of blinders. I lost in short order about $200,000. That was almost everything I had and I was forced to start over at the age of 46. However, the experience quite literally got me back *On Course*. It brought me back into studying the Course at a deeper level than ever before. The loss of everything external forced me to look inside to find out what is really valuable. So it is for anyone when misfortune becomes fortune. In a similar way, I have a friend who has AIDS. He says that his experience has forced him to look at his own mortality and thus also brought him closer to God.

As things are taken from us we recognize more clearly what is truly valuable and what is valueless. When things are taken from us we have already recognized someplace in our mind their worthlessness. We also may not be able to make the shift entirely internally so we need a stimulus to turn our gaze within (M-4. I.(A). 3:5).

2. A Period of Sorting Out

After undoing there comes a period of sorting out. Now that we have either *chosen* or have *seemingly been forced* to let go of the unessential, we are now in a position to decide what is really valuable, what helps and what hampers. My experience in the loss of the inn was a general loss of interest in material things. I still have a passing interest in antiques, though I no longer buy and sell them with the same fascination as I once did. This is not a judgment of those who buy and sell antiques. Each of us must embrace some enjoyable way of making our way through the world, making a living as we go, but for me playing with antiques became a distraction. It was taking up my time and keeping me from the work I was called to do. In the section of the *Manual for Teachers* entitled "How should a teacher of God spend his day?" it says:

Routines as such are dangerous,
because they easily become gods in their own right,
threatening the very goals for which they were set up.
M-16. 2:5

Anything we do repetitively, daily or unconsciously can be a distraction that takes us away from God. Dropping habits that hamper our progress lightens our load and speeds the process of spiritual development.

3. The Period of Relinquishment

It is not surprising that we must relinquish the past to gain something new. We must release the nonessential to gain the essential. We need to give up what we do not want and keep what we do (M-4. I.(A). 6:6-7). If we think that we are giving up something *desirable,* this experience will engender conflict. I was talking with a Course leader from California who told me that the deeper he got into the Course, the fewer things of this world held his attention. This is not to say that we should not enjoy our relationships, our various hobbies, going to movies, eating out or any recreational activities. However, the more rewarding the spiritual journey, the less fascination one finds with what the Course calls the trifling treasures, trinkets and toys of this world. There is nothing more interesting than the spiritual journey. Once we have set our feet on the path nothing of the world can nourish our souls except to continue to explore the path to God as it opens up before us. Learning is a happy experience when it leads us along our natural path while facilitating the unfolding of who we already are (T-8. II. 2:7).

I sold the inn for $100,000 less than I had paid for it and it left me with a marvelously clean feeling. I had lost everything, financially speaking, but I was also freed of a gigantic white elephant that had taken my time, my interests, my energies, and most importantly, my peace of mind. There is a Japanese poem that goes:

> *My barn having burned to the ground*
> *I can now see the moon.*

4. A Period of Settling Down

We need this period of rest because the journey is not over. As the initial goal has been achieved, however, we can rest for a while. Now we consolidate our learning, realizing that this is the way out. Now we see why it was we went the way we did in order to learn what we needed to learn.

> "Give up what you do not want,
> and keep what you do."
> How simple is the obvious!
> And how easy to do!
> M-4.I(A). 6:6-8

Those who have overcome various addictions, after they have been free from the addiction for a time, may wonder why it was ever such a challenge in the first place. Once it is truly gone, once it is in the past—it is in the past, and has nothing to do with present reality. Now we can move ahead again without so many distractions that previously pulled us off course. Now do we move ahead with deeper guidance. During this time we can also bring the other characteristics of a teacher of God more clearly into our lives.

5. A Period of Unsettling

We have learned the importance of sorting out the valuable from the valueless and the importance of letting go of that which we do not need. Now we must rely only on the guidance of the Holy Spirit. This is a difficult lesson and the next step is *a period of unsettling*. Now do we learn that there is no sacrifice, for what we seem to have lost along the way has been nothing at all. You lose nothing when you lose an illusion. Thinking we had to make a sacrifice got in the way. For this reason we fear death, thinking we are going to have to give up all we have built along the way. There is, however, nothing to sacrifice.

Now is the time to get serious; no more part-time teaching, part-time failing, part-time succeeding. Now we step out of our comfort zone, focus our attention on the direction we need to go, lay all judgment aside and ask only what God wants in every circumstance. To be in the Kingdom simply requires the focusing of our complete attention on it (T-7. III. 3:7).

6. The Period of Achievement

Finally, what before were shadows become solid gains. Learning is consolidated in honest absorption, consistency of thought and full transfer (M-4. I.(A). 8:3). This is the real world, the stage of real peace, for now Heaven is not something ahead of us. Heaven is here and Heaven is now. Even when seeming "emergencies" confront us, our peace is not lost nor even shaken and we know how to respond. We go through these stages to deepen our trust in God and reliance upon His direction. The less we need the ego and the more we turn to God, the easier it is to be one of His teachers.

Oliver Cromwell's secretary was sent to Europe on some important business. He stayed one night at a seaport town and tossed on his bed, unable to sleep. A servant who was with him in the same room was sleeping soundly. The secretary at length awakened his servant and asked how he could sleep so soundly while he himself could not. The servant asked his master why he could not sleep and he said he was afraid something might go wrong in his meeting with the French Monarch.

"Master," said the valet, "may I ask a question or two?"

"To be sure."

"Did God rule the universe before we were born?"

"Most assuredly He did."

"And will He rule it after we are dead?"

"Certainly He will."

"Then, master, why not let Him rule the present, too?"

Trusting in the petty leads of our egos is trusting in nothing. By trusting in God we let him rule the present too.

Dolores once told me of the experience of washing Sarah's hair. Sarah would sit in the bathtub while she put shampoo on her hair. Then, when she poured on the water to make a lather, Sarah would tip her head down so that the shampoo ran into her eyes, causing pain and tears. Dolores explained that if she just looked straight up at her, she could avoid getting shampoo in her face. Sarah would agree; then, as soon as Dolores started to rinse her hair, Sarah's fear would overcome her trust, and she would look down again. Naturally the shampoo would run into Sarah's eyes again, and there would be more tears.

This situation is rather like our relationship to God. God is our Father who loves us. We are to place all of our trust in Him. However, the ego does not trust and in difficult situations it panics and looks down. This never solves the problem. We just become more afraid and the "shampoo" blinds us. Often in the Bible we are told to lift up our heads to God when problems come. He knows how to protect us if we remember to listen to Him. Trust is the first and most basic law of happiness. The individual who intends to succeed in liberating themselves from fear and delusion has to find a way to trust. Trust is the first portal that everyone *must* pass through in order to discover themselves. First, we *must* place our trust in His strength by accepting His gifts rather than relying on the resources of the ego.

I will trust, and not be afraid.
Isaiah 12:2

Chapter 6

The Law of Honesty

You never find yourself until you face the truth.
Pearl Bailey

A miracle contains the gift of grace,
for it is given and received as one.
And thus it illustrates the law of truth the world does not obey,
because it fails entirely to understand its ways.
A miracles inverts perception which was upside down before,
and thus it ends the strange distortions that were manifest.
Now is perception open to the truth.
Now is forgiveness seen as justified.
W-pII. 13.2:1-5

Pilate therefore said to him, "Are you a king?" Then Jesus
answered, "It is you who say it. Yes, I am a king. I was born for this.
I came into the world for this; to bear witness to the truth; and all
who are on the side of truth listen to my voice."
"Truth?" said Pilate, "What is that?"
John 18: 37-38

The second characteristic of a teacher of God is honesty.
Honesty is based on trust as the trusting can afford honesty. Trust is a
preface to honesty as we tell the truth to those we trust. Trust is also a
preface to love. By trusting and speaking the truth, love also comes
along. It is automatic. It is not something we have to work on. Love
will follow after truth, but truth will not always follow after what *we
think* is love. In the movie *Camellia* the heroine turns to her lover
who has just declared his love for her and says, "Well, love me less
or understand me better."

- Understanding is the important thing.
- Honesty is the important thing.

- Letting the other person be who they are is the important thing.

Life Without Lies

There is a scene in the first Superman movie with Christopher Reeve and Margot Kidder where Superman is flying around with Lois Lane. They come back and land on her balcony. Lois Lane stares into Superman's eyes—it is a romantic moment with the promise of a kiss. Then Lois says, "Superman, what do you believe in?" Superman looks her straight in the eye and says, "I believe in truth, justice and the American way." To which Lois Lane replies, "You've got to be kidding." Superman responds, "Lois, I never lie." Although Superman never lies, his alter ego Clark Kent lies frequently, claiming that he has no knowledge of Superman. Similarly, each of us lies insofar as we do not give testimony to our true reality but speak instead of our belief in illusion.

One of the most obvious contradictions of life is that while we profess a reverence for honesty, we frequently disregard the practice. It is not uncommon for any one of us to decide to deprive another of the truth *for their own sake*, whether they like it or not.

There is a story of a minister who notices a group of boys standing around a small stray dog and asks:
"What are you boys doing?"
"Telling lies," said one of the boys.
"The one who tells the biggest lie gets the dog."
"Why, when I was your age," the minister said, "I never thought of telling a lie."
The boys looked at one another a little downcast and one of them said: "I guess you win the dog."

We've all been hiding a lot more than we are willing to admit. Lying is so frequently used that we do it without conscious awareness and almost no one is free of it. *Time* magazine once ran a cover story with its lead article entitled "Lying: Everybody Is Doing It." Let's admit that we each have a secret life. As Billy Graham once expressed it: "Everybody has a little bit of Watergate in him." I read with great interest Dr. Brad Blanton's book: *Radical Honesty: How To Transform Your Life By Telling the Truth.* Dr. Blanton talks about a survey in which respondents were guaranteed anonymity. One of the questions was about lying. 93% of the respondents said they lied regularly and habitually; he was wondering if, maybe, the remaining 7% were the biggest liars of all.

This is the way Dr. Blanton begins his book:

"I am fifty-three years old. I have been a psychotherapist in Washington, D.C. for 25 years. People come to my office and pay me money to pay attention to them and I do what I can to help out. I have some skill in helping people find ways to make their lives work.

"This is what I have learned:

"*We all lie like hell.* It wears us out. It is *the* major source of human stress. Lying kills people.

"The kind of lying that is most deadly is withholding, or keeping back information from someone we think would be affected by it. Psychological illness of the severest kind is the result of this kind of lying. Psychological healing is possible only with the freedom that comes from not hiding anymore. Keeping secrets and hiding from other people is a trap. Adolescents spend most of their time playing this hide-and-seek game. The better you are at getting by with playing hide-and-seek during adolescence, the harder it is to grow up. Important secrets and all the plotting and cogitation that go with them are all bullshit."

Nations deliberately deceive other nations. Espionage, spying, concealment and secretiveness are so much a part of international affairs, so much a part of business relationships and church politics, that we don't even think it is unnatural. Two Hollywood executives are talking to one another and one of them says, "You're lying to me." To which the other responds, "I know. But, hear me out."

Hiding

The first thing that Adam does after he has eaten of the fruit of the tree of good and evil (the symbol of division in consciousness) is hide. When God finds him He wants to know why he is hiding and Adam says it is because he is naked. Where there was unity there are now two possibilities, good and evil. The thought of the possibility of being able to think a thought outside of the mind of God is so offensive to Adam that he must hide his nakedness — his shame, his guilt. Actually nothing has happened. We cannot do anything against God. We cannot hurt God. Adam, in fear, goes and hides and we are all still hiding. If we weren't hiding, we would know that we are one with God.

There is no one among us who has not lied, who has not been thoughtless, apathetic and condemning of others. Each of us has been selfish, pushy, arrogant and rude. Each of us has had the occasion to lose our tempers. We cheat on our income tax or we cheat in line, or we have cut off other drivers who are just as delayed as we are. We all have or have had secret lives of selfishness, desires, appetites, passions, fantasies and lusts. We've all been envious, suspicious and jealous of others. There have been times in which we have not only not wished our neighbor well but have wished him ill.

> Nothing brings quite so much satisfaction
> as the failure of a friend.
> Mark Twain

There is a sad truth in Mark Twain's quote. We are quick to attack our brothers and sisters and we've all harbored murderous thoughts, maybe not overtly, but there have probably been times when each of us has wished someone dead.

> Attack in any form is equally destructive.
> Its purpose does not change. Its sole intent is murder,
> and what form of murder serves to cover the massive guilt
> and frantic fear of punishment the murderer must feel?
> No one thinks of murder and escapes the guilt the thought entails.
> T-23.III. 1:3-5&8

By accepting into our mind the idea of separation we are condemning our own identity to death:

• We are afraid to learn the Course, for we are afraid that it will mean our ego's undoing, which is exactly what it does mean.
• We are afraid redemption is going to kill us and being saved will be our demise.

Psychologists use the word *complex* or *coex* to describe complicated places in the psyche where we are hung up, attached, not free, not truthful. Complexes are complicated, secret webs in which we catch nothing but ourselves. Our building up of a world of complexity is the ego's attempt to obscure the obvious (T-15.IV. 6:2). While complexity is of the ego the truth is simple and must be taught to those who lose their way in endless mazes of complexity (P-2.V.1:1). It's been said of the Course that it is simple but not easy. Honesty is a simple thing that may seem hard, but once we've practiced it, it's so freeing we wonder why we've not been doing it all along.

Hiding, or Keeping Things to Ourselves

For the ego, salvation lies in keeping things to itself. Yet, in hiding, we shut off communication. We cannot accept perfect communication as long as we hide it from ourselves. For what we hide is hidden from us (T-15.IV. 9:6&7). While lying may seem like the usual, and therefore natural choice, it is unnatural. "Miracles are natural. When they do not occur something has gone wrong" (T-1.I.6:1&2). True vision is the natural perception (5-3.III.4:1). Lying, as a means of hiding, blocks awareness of inner guidance. The problem is not that the Holy Spirit is absent. The Holy Spirit is very present. It is we who are absent. And we are unaware of the presence of the Holy Spirit to the degree that we hide from Him and thus ourselves.

As ego beings we make many illusions for ourselves. Society helps by reinforcing a host of illusory mores, principles, laws and false proverbs. Illusions are fed to us with amazing care by the psychologists of Madison Avenue, righteous evangelists, paranoid generals, and the various corporations for whom we work.

Your Guilty Secret

The ego needs tools for defense and seeks to build a world of its own where it can keep its secrets hidden from God and everyone else. The problem is that the more we fortify our own world with secrets, the deeper our sense of separation. God is always immediately at hand, but if we've built up a powerful, complex system of defense it's hard to know Him.

The Depth of Our Guilt

Our guilt is greater than most of us are willing to recognize. A friend, Gary Gross, had gone to one of Ken Wapnick's workshops and listened to him talk about guilt. Gary could not think of anything about which he felt guilty and said so, to which Ken responded, "You don't feel guilty—shame on you!" This response brought an uproar of laughter. Each of us have far more guilt buried within us than we are willing to look at. The first defense of the ego is denial. To say there is nothing about which we feel guilty is simply, usually, just to overlook that which we do not want to look at, for to do so would just be too much for us. Yet it is only in looking that we can be free.

"*Guilt is* a sure sign that your thinking is unnatural."

T-5.V. 4:2

"*Guilt is* inescapable by those who believe they order their own thoughts and must therefore obey their dictates." T-5. V. 7:6

"*Guilt. . . is* a way of holding past and future in your minds to ensure the ego's continuity." T-13. I. 8:6

"*Guilt is* the condition of sacrifice, as peace is the condition for the awareness of your relationship with God." T-15. XI. 4:3

"*Guilt is* the only need the ego has, and as long as you identify with it, guilt will remain attractive to you." T-15. VII. 10:4

"*Guilt is always* disruptive." T-5. V. 2:6

"*Guilt* remains the only thing that hides the Father, for guilt is the attack upon His Son." T-13. IX. 1:1

"*Guilt cannot* last when the idea of sacrifice has been removed." T-15. X. 5:11

"*Guilt asks* for punishment, and its request is granted."

T-26. VII. 3:1

(Emphasis added in the above quotes.)

Why Lie?

All lying comes out of fear. Being afraid, we think we need protection. It is thus the case that: Under each cornerstone of fear on which we erect our insane systems of belief the truth lies hidden (T-14.VII.2:7). All fear comes from the ego. To be ego-endowed means to live with lies, even simple lies of omission in which we do not tell *everything* to our employer or employees, friends, children, parents, or spouses. We are afraid to do so for *fear* that we will lose

66

our job, prestige, power, or money, or that we will not be understood, or that someone will be angry with us or leave us.

The First Lie

Lying is one of the first defenses a child learns. Can you remember the first time you lied? Probably not, because it was so long ago that you can hardly get to it, but chances are you lied to your mother first. Lying to mother is like lying to God. It is the thing that got us into this pickle of separated consciousness.

One day when I was a young man, I was working down in the barn when I heard my mother yelling my name way back up at the house. I tore out of the barn and up to the house thinking she had been hurt. As it turned out she had, but it was an emotional not a physical hurt, and *I* was the culprit. I went running to her as she came running to me. We met in the middle and she opened her hand to reveal two half smoked cigarette butts she had found in my jeans pocket. She had the goods on me, so I confessed that Clifford Mongler and I had tried them out but did not like them. That is why we had put them out without completely smoking them. Actually, we had only smoked them half way as we thought we heard someone coming and put them out before we got caught.

We begin lying when we are very young. We do it because we are afraid. As parents, it therefore behooves us to tell the truth to children and to learn how to ask questions in such a way that children are more likely to tell the truth. If you say, "You wouldn't lie to me, would you?" You are almost certain to be lied to. That's like one mate saying to another, "You wouldn't be unfaithful to me, would you?" Such rhetorical questions demand a negative answer. If you say, "Yes, I would lie to you," or "Yes, I would be unfaithful to you," you are in for it. If you were to say that, you would probably be clobbered orally if not physically. And who wants to be clobbered? Or, how about, "You'd better not be lying to me!" Do you think this will bring a confession?

Hypocrisy—Play Acting

I was a Methodist minister for 28 years but the Methodist church and I came to a parting of the ways in 1989. I now realize that had I been more honest with the Methodist church and myself earlier, things would have worked out much more smoothly. I would have left the church sooner and would thus have avoided much pain and frustration.

There never was any doubt in my mind about my calling to the ministry. I never seriously considered any other profession except teaching. Though I was employed in the ministry, there were many aspects of Methodism in particular and Protestantism in general that I did not agree with. Yet I went along because I needed a job and I had a theological degree. This was a form of lying. The more I was there, the more I didn't want to be and the more I did not want to be there, the more the hierarchy did not want me there. The frustration fed on itself. I wanted to be a minister but I was not having fun trying to fit into what I increasingly came to experience as an inflexible and rigid format. In order to go along I had to compromise, and in that compromising there were many lies. I was progressively thinking more globally and eclectically than the Methodist church. Still, I tried to fit into a pattern that was uncomfortable and painful. Living this way meant living with a certain amount of unpleasant hypocrisy.

The word *hypocrisy* comes from the Greek *hypocrisies*, which means *play-acting* or *pretense*. I had to pretend and in that pretense was dishonesty. Because I wanted a job as a minister, and as it had not occurred to me that I could quit and start my own church, I compromised and went along and continued to be frustrated. My experience with the Methodist church is similar to that of many people caught in corporate structures who think they must play the game and try to do so without success. The truth is, that in all such cases, telling the truth will either improve our position in the company (because our truth telling will be regarded as refreshingly innovative) or it will help us to get promoted out of the organization. Either way, it brings us more authenticity, integrity and ultimately, greater happiness. If we look at the truth of who we really are and what we really want, and if we stick up for that, we will get it.

If you tell the truth, you don't have to remember anything.
Mark Twain

Setting the False Aside

We overcome guilt by looking at the truth, but the truth is the last thing we want to look at for we think it would just be too terrible. If you are to retain guilt, as the ego insists, *you cannot be you* (T-13.II.1:3). And what do you or I want more than to be ourselves? Moving more deeply into accepting the Course, I've realized how my own self-absorption has dominated my life and how much easier life would have been without such a narrow focus. It does no good to wallow in the past. Jerry Jampolsky says that "Forgiveness of ourselves comes in recognizing that we could never have another past." Honesty requires self-examination, and the deeper we look the less we may like what we see. Looking deeply, however, can also motivate us to change.

To try to dedicate ourselves both to truth and illusion is impossible. *Truth is the absence of illusion and illusion is the absence of truth. Both cannot be together* (T-19.I.5:8-11). This world and all we have built in it is false. That does not mean it is bad. It simply means that we just need to refuse to be part of a fearful dream. Then truth moves to the foreground and we are set free.

What the Truth Is Not

The only way to speak the truth is to do so lovingly.
Henry David Thoreau

Honesty does not involve telling someone off. It's not giving someone a piece of our mind or telling them what we think of them. If *you think* your girlfriend is wearing an ugly dress that's just your opinion. It is not the truth. What is in *fashion* is not what is true. Our *opinions* or *beliefs* are not the truth. *The cruel truth is not the truth.* Telling someone what we think of them may seem like the truth but *look who's talking.* We are to remind our brothers of who they are, *not* who they are not. We are to look as the Holy Spirit looks, and understand as He understands. The Holy Spirit is always in communion with God. He is also part of us. The Holy Spirit is our guide to salvation, because He holds the remembrance of things past and to come, and brings them to the present (T-5.III. 11:6,8&9).

How can we get free of the difficulties associated with lying? How do we get to that wonderful freedom where truth pervades our lives? The first step is in sorting out the false from the true. Being aware of the blocks to love's presence and learning to choose another teacher produces miracles. We are afraid of the truth because we are afraid it is going to hurt. But like surgery, if it hurts at all, it's only for a moment. Like surgery, it also cures. Truth speaking or *catharsis* is a form of purification or cleansing.

A Test for Truth

First we have to recognize that we do not know what the truth is. Based upon our ego experience, all that we know has not given us the truth. We may have many ideas about what truth is but, insofar as these ideas are based on our fears and anxieties, they tell us nothing. The task of the miracle worker is thus *to deny the denial of truth* (T-12. II. 1:5). We are not to affirm truth. On an ego level we do not know what the truth is. Our task is to remove the blocks to the awareness of truth, not to impede progress by setting up more blocks.

> You are as sick as your secrets.
> Alcoholics Anonymous saying

Those who have been through any of the Anonymous programs such as—Alcoholics Anonymous, Narcotics Anonymous, Gamblers Anonymous, etc.—will tell you how free they felt once they were no longer hiding. At that point they can also see that their addiction is, in fact, not the truth of who they really are.

We come to truth as we relinquish illusion. In *Pilgrim's Progress*, the hero, Christian, begins his journey to Heaven with a number of burdens on his back. He goes through a series of painful, but necessary, experiences all designed to help him let go of his burdens. The burdens had such names as greed, pride, deceit and selfishness. They were the blocks that were keeping him from an awareness of inner guidance and his own true happiness.

Purification may appear painful, but it is inevitably freeing. During the time I worked as a college professor inside the New York State prison system I noted that many of my students had to admit to a seemingly cruel truth by taking responsibility for their actions. They had to admit the truth even when it meant going to prison.

Looking at the truth *now,* means being free *now.* If we can be free *now* we can experience Heaven *now.*

Now let's take a long, hard look at ourselves. Let's *confess, acknowledge* and *recognize* the darkness that we feel is lurking within. If we want to be free, we're going to have to demonstrate a little willingness to dig deeper and actually look at our guilty secrets. These are the blocks which keep us from an awareness of love's presence. I'm not suggesting that we hang our dirty laundry out to dry nor am I suggesting that we offer up a public confession. There is, however, much that we could do to bring us to the truth.

1. Take It to the Holy Spirit

First, take your guilty secrets to the Holy Spirit. This means to be willing to be honest with ourselves. The Holy Spirit would have us bring to Him everything we keep hidden. The Holy Spirit can bring light to darkness but we have to open the way for Him. What we hide, He cannot bring light to. Unless we look with Him what is in darkness remains in darkness.

Bring, therefore, all your dark and secret thoughts to Him,
and look upon them with Him.
He holds the light, and you the darkness.
They cannot coexist when Both of you together look on them.
His judgment must prevail,
and He will give it to you as you join your perception to His.
T-14. VII. 6:8-11

To recognize darkness is to give it up. To look at it is to do something about it. As we offer up to the Holy Spirit all our guilty secrets and say: "Help me to see the truth in this problem," a new reality becomes possible. This is a liberating experience. I was impressed in watching Rev. Jim Baker's interview with Barbara Walters. Here is a man who had to face the truth. He has written an autobiography of himself entitled *I Was Wrong.* The interview struck me as refreshingly open, honest and forthright.

2. Take It to a Loving Friend or Therapist

It is helpful to consider sharing some seemingly dark secrets with a good friend or caring therapist who will be willing to hear us out. This is where the benefits in programs like Alcoholics Anonymous come in, as there is an opportunity to look at one's darkness in an accepting atmosphere. Such a process can be refreshing, especially if we then change the way we look at things. Taking responsibility means we no longer blame outside circumstances, other people or past events for the conditions of our own life.

When we are about to hide something it is helpful to ask ourselves if we really need to and see if we can be more honest. Certainly we are going to feel much better if we do. What are the things we seek to keep secret? Why is it that we cannot tell the truth to someone? Anyone? Why be so divisive? Why can't we tell the truth? What would happen if we did? When tempted to lie it is helpful to look at the lie for a moment and then go ahead and speak the truth even if it means being a little embarrassed, even if it makes me seem a little stupid. It is better to be ignorant than dishonest.

3. Asking for Forgiveness

It is also a good idea to go to anyone we feel we have hurt and ask for forgiveness. We are then in a position to do something positive with our lives. Confession frees us from arrogance. It is impossible to remember God alone and in secret. Remembering Him means we are not alone (T-14. X. 10:1&2).

God has no secret communications,
for everything of Him is perfectly open
and freely accessible to all, being for all.
Nothing lives in secret,
and what you would hide from the Holy Spirit is nothing.
T- 14. X. 11:2&3

The escape from darkness involves two stages:
1. The recognition that darkness cannot hide, which usually entails fear.
2. The recognition that there is nothing we want to hide, which brings escape from fear.

In looking deeper, we discover that the places we thought were so terrible are not so terrible. First of all, we all harbor these feelings. Secondly, by looking at them in the light, we take away their shadowy power and their unconscious dominance over us.

Granting exposure to dark places loosens the ego's grip. By becoming more aware of our deceit and the places we have been hurtful, we gain some control over such thoughts and actions. Dr. Blanton talks about *using the mind rather than being used by the mind,* which is similar to the Course's talking about mind training, or discovering the power of choice that we have to change our minds and switch from wrong-minded to right-minded thinking.

> Your *guilty secret* is nothing,
> and if you will but bring it to the light,
> the Light will dispel it.
> And then no dark cloud will remain between you
> and the remembrance of your Father . . .
> T-13. II. 9:2&3

If the truth, the whole truth, and nothing but the truth seems too frightening then start in a simple way. Start anyplace where it will be helpful. If we can let a little of the truth in, then we can create greater space for more truth.

Dolores and I occasionally say to each other, "Is there anything you haven't told me?" We often find some little something we can share with each other at that point. Perhaps some little fear or anxiety. Sharing it takes the energy away from it. It is also helpful to have a brother's or sister's feedback. Sometimes they can see the way out of a problem that has eluded us.

Honesty is a small thing that can be great and noble. If the whole truth seems too terrible to look at, begin by letting a small piece of truth in. Tell the truth and don't worry about being clobbered. A little willingness is called for, a bit of willingness to simply let be what already is.

1. *Tell the truth about the past.* It's helpful to tell the truth about something which may have seemed a big deal in the past but no longer is in the forefront of consciousness as a major issue.

2. Drop exaggerations, embellishments and overstatements, such as how long it took to do something, how far we traveled or how hard we had to work on a project. Why would we ever exaggerate or embellish anything unless we either wanted to impress someone or hide something?

3. It is helpful to notice when we are tempted to lie about even the smallest thing. When someone asks a question, about what we have read or how familiar we are with certain ideas, there may be a temptation to say, "Yes I know about that" or "I read that." Admitting that we don't know something is more refreshing than pretending that we do know.

4. When tempted to lie about even the smallest thing, it's helpful for us to ask ourselves if we really need to. Do we really need to be so afraid? The greater our fear, the more likely we will hide. The more we trust, the more we can speak the truth without fear. Other people are also ready for miracles and are more accepting of our truth than we may think. Truth speaking is refreshing and rejuvenating.

5. Trust that telling the truth will be okay, for it will be okay.

If in doubt, tell the truth.
Mark Twain

Tell the truth as fast as you can.
Bob Mandel

Relax in the hands of God, knowing that in God's hands everything is okay. We only have to give up something *we think* we need. The more truth we admit to, the easier life will get and the less separated we will feel. When we tell the truth we feel better about ourselves and destiny opens up in accordance with our own greatest happiness. This is freedom. Honesty not only applies to what we say. Honesty means consistency, coherence and congruity. When we are honest there is nothing we say that contradicts what we think. The ego mind in opposition to God is inconsistency itself.

Such are the truly honest.
At no level are they in conflict with themselves.

Therefore it is impossible for them to be in conflict
with anyone or anything.
M-4.II.1:7&8

If I am not at peace then I have *chosen* not to be at peace. I have chosen to be at war with God. In perfect honesty there is no war. At one with ourselves there is no conflict. If we are conflicted with ourselves we are conflicted with those with whom we cannot share the truth. Lying, hiding, cheating all make us unhappy and foster the separation we have between ourselves and others. *It is a law of happiness that we cannot be happy and deceptive at the same time.* Happiness comes in living a life which is free, clear and clean. We stay free, clear and clean by telling the truth. We are happy to the degree to which we are free and we are free to the degree to which we do not hide.

Once illusion goes, Truth must take its place. Ultimately all Truth will be known. *Ultimately* can be now, tomorrow, or at the hour of our death. To know the Truth is to step into Eternity and allow Eternity to enter into our lives. The little inadequacies that clutter our lives are not who we really are. We cannot advance into the Kingdom as long as we tenaciously hang on to petty concerns and little fears. The ego tries to persuade us that it is up to us to decide which voice is true. The Holy Spirit teaches us that what was created by God is wholly true, and our decision making cannot change it.

It is possible to get increasingly clear about our purpose. Our purpose is forgiveness and our destiny is to accept the Atonement for ourselves. It comes as we drop:
- the illusion of the ego.
- the illusion that we are bodies.
- the fear—to tell the truth to anyone.
- the junk we do not need.
- the burdens we need not carry.

The truth is we are already free but aren't aware of freedom's presence. The reflection of truth is always available to us if we are just willing to accept it.

Heaven, by definition, is a place where Truth is. Heaven, by definition, is free. In our experience of time, in our seeming involvement and entrapment in the complex world of the ego, truth may become fuzzy, glossed over and blurry, but it doesn't have to be. At any moment, any one of us could wake up and recognize the Truth of our identity as sons and daughters of God. In Truth, we are all teachers of God and it is our function to speak the Truth. The sooner we accept our function, the happier we will be.

Honesty cannot hurt. In fact, it's a great relief. Defenses are not necessary. Illusions are not necessary. Getting on with looking at the ego and choosing a different teacher, we can be free right now. We could experience Heaven now. Heaven is the Truth. It is the only Truth there is. At any moment, any one of us can know the Truth and the Truth will make us free.

> The peace of mind which the advanced teachers of God experience
> is largely due to their perfect honesty.
> It is only the wish to deceive that makes for war.
> M-4.II. 2:1&2

Only What Is Loving Is True
There really isn't any choice about telling the truth. All darkness will and must be brought to light so it might as well be disclosed, looked at, perceived now. Joining the Atonement is the way out of fear. Everything we perceive as fearful, the Holy Spirit will help us reinterpret and teach us that only what is loving is true. Truth is beyond our ability to destroy, but entirely within our ability to accept (T-5. IV. 1:3&4). Choosing for the Holy Spirit, we also choose for God. This task is not terrible or onerous and it is not ours alone. Opening up to beauty is a matter of coming to the truth. The world is full of beauty when the heart is full of love.

> This above all—to thine own self be true,
> and it must follow, as night the day,
> thou canst not then be false to any man.
> William Shakespeare

Chapter 7

The Law of Tolerance

Judge not, that you be not judged.
For with the judgment you pronounce you will be judged,
and the measure you give will be the measure you get.
Why do you see the speck that is in your brother's eye,
but do not notice the log that is in your own eye?
Or how can you say to your brother,
"Let me take the speck out of your eye,"
when there is a log in your own eye?
. . . first take the log out of your own eye,
and then you will see clearly
how to take the speck out of your brother's eye.
Matthew 7:1-4

The third characteristic of a teacher of God is tolerance. Although the section heading is entitled tolerance, the word tolerance only appears four times in the whole Course. Our concern is thus with *judgment, projection, condemnation* and *attack.*

I had just finished performing a wedding ceremony and was walking along 81st Street and Central Park West in New York City opposite the building where Judy Skutch lived back during the 1970s. This was one of the places where I would occasionally meet Helen Schucman. I stopped for a moment, looking up at the corner apartments counting up to the fifth floor where Judy used to live. While I stood there an older couple approached me talking fairly brazenly to each other. As they got closer I could hear he was saying to her, "You are wrong," to which she responded, "No, you are wrong." And then she gave some reason, after which he responded, "No, you are wrong," and he gave some reason. I looked at their faces. Each was quite obviously feeling justified in what they were saying, and each of them was angry. Here was a couple of obviously advanced age fighting with each other quite ardently.

What does it mean to be tolerant?
Tolerance does not mean:
- the capacity to endure hardship
- allowing unacceptable behavior, say on the part of a child
- simply *to tolerate* someone

Tolerance means:
- the absence of judgment
- the practice of respecting others
- seeing no differences

The Nature of Judgment

Judgment implies that there is something to choose between. When Adam bit into the fruit of the knowledge of *good* and *evil*, and a split entered into the mind, suddenly a *seeming* choice presented itself. Choice exists only in a world of separation. Judgment is separation. As there is no separation in Heaven, there is no judgment in Heaven. There are no choices that have to be made—no division.

Perhaps you think that different kinds of love are possible.
Perhaps you think there is a kind of love for this,
a kind for that; a way of loving one,
another way of loving still another.
Love is one.
It has no separated parts and no degrees;
no kinds nor levels, no divergences and no distinctions.
W-pI.127. 1:1-4

Love is one. Heaven is one. God is one. If we are all one, there can be no judgment. Only the ego can judge. Only the ego thinks that judgment is called for. The Course is asking us to become aware of the fact that we are in a constant state of judgment.

Obviously it is necessary for us to make a number of judgments in this world: "What am I going to wear today?" "What would I like to eat for lunch or dinner?" "Which movie should I go see?" Not making judgments does not mean not making decisions in this world. It means not making a big deal of decisions and not attacking or condemning others. What kind of clothes to wear is no big deal, unless you are into power dressing or dressing to

78

manipulate, in which case deciding what you are going to wear is an *attack.*

We simply need to be aware of those times when our judgments have ego thoughts associated with them, which is most of the time. When the Course says not to judge, it does not mean to deny that differences exist in the world. The nature of the ego is to separate, segregate, compare, analyze, interpret, project and judge. It is also the nature of the ego to defend. Therefore, even the smallest judgment against us is perceived as an attack and the natural response is to defend by attacking back. The ego is very fragile and extremely volatile. We are easily hurt and offended. We think that we can correct other people. We think that if we just tell them off once and for all they will "get it" and shape up. It never happens! As it is the nature of the ego to defend, all we get when we tell people off is increasing defensiveness.

Projection—First, Remove the Log
We cannot judge without projecting. Projection reinterprets our guilt, telling us that what seems to be our guilt really belongs to someone else, so we blame someone else in order to escape blaming ourselves. Projection is the process of ascribing to others our own ideas and impulses. When we project we take our problem and say, "The problem is not mine. It is yours." Projection means: *to hurl away.* So, we choose someone whom we can make responsible for how we feel and cast our feelings out onto them. We then separate ourselves from that person either directly or psychologically. We place distance between ourselves and others and then say it is the other who is evil, cold and judgmental. We can then feel justified in attacking them for whatever we project onto them.

Jesus tells us to turn the other cheek. He told Peter to put away his sword. He says that those who live by the sword will die by the sword.

Projection and attack are inevitably related,
because projection is always a means of justifying attack.
Anger without projection is impossible.
T-6. II. 3:5&6

79

Though ostensibly aimed at the outside world, attack is inevitably a judgment against ourselves. We cannot help feeling guilt for our projections. We feel worse and so does the one we attack. From the ego's point of view, the object of our intolerance doesn't matter. We often project onto the ones closest to us. For this reason there are many abused children, wives, and husbands. We attack whomever we can make responsible for the unpleasantness we feel—whoever left the house in a mess—whoever else has not fulfilled his responsibility. When God catches up with Adam and Eve in the Garden, Adam says, *Eve made me do it.* Then God looks at Eve, who says, *The serpent (devil) made me do it.* Projection stands at the very beginning of the ego's development.

The Secret Wish to Be Victimized

On an ego level we actually enjoy being victimized, abandoned and betrayed because this proves beyond a shadow of a doubt that we are innocent victims of what other people did to us. Our lives are the perfect expression of this unconscious wish. Each of us has a formidable investment in being unfairly treated. If you can be really honest you will see that there is a part of each of us that enjoys being hurt.

Beware of the temptation to perceive yourself unfairly treated.
T-26. X. 4:1

The only time Jesus asks us to *beware,* in the entire Course, is in the above statement. This is the great temptation of the world. Dr. Wapnick says we made up the world so we would be unfairly treated. There is no one of us who gets all the love and attention we want in this world, at least not all the time. Most of us do not get the love and attention we think we deserve. We thus set up the world for ourselves in such a way as to prove that we are innocent victims. If we are really honest with ourselves we can recognize that there is a secret delight in suffering because our suffering is proof of the fact that somebody has hurt us. We can therefore blame someone else for our misfortune. We did not do it to ourselves—so somebody did it to us. Thus, when we pray to the Holy Spirit we need to ask not that the circumstances of our lives be changed but that we be given the opportunity to look at things differently.

Seeing ourselves as victims who have been unfairly treated is a simple, natural defense. But it does not work. It does not speak to our majesty. It speaks to our dreaming. It speaks of our illusion. We cannot be unfairly treated, and believing that we can be is but another form of the idea that we are deprived by someone else. We have no enemy except ourselves (T-26. X. 3:2,3&6).

In Matthew 10:30 Jesus says, "A man's enemies are those of his own house." Jesus is not talking about our brothers and sisters. He's talking about ourselves. In telling the world how badly we've been treated and how we suffer at the hands of others, we make ourselves sick. We make ourselves sick by backing further and further into guilt through our projections. In the Carlos Castaneda series, Don Juan tells his student, Carlos, that *he doesn't know anything* because he is constantly rehearsing his problems with his family and friends. Rehashing our problems keeps us from seeing. It keeps us from freedom.

Why Aren't We Happy?

As we look at all the things that bring us pain, the one thing we overlook is our guilt. It is the last thing we want to recognize. We do not recognize we are making illusions while we are making them. We think our illusions are quite real, thus we can justify attack.

The fundamentalist believes that he is quite right in his perceptions and his projections. Therefore, he has every right to destroy his opposition, whom he perceives as a personification of the devil. So some New Age fundamentalists dig underground bomb shelters and buy guns; Prime Minister Yitzhak Rabin is assassinated and buildings are blown up—all in the name of God.

There is a bit of fundamentalism in all of us and we think we are right and justified in our projections. Thus we give our illusions power over us. As long as I think that my suffering comes from the outside world, I must be a victim and experience myself as deprived, and lacking in love. As long as we see ourselves as victims, we will believe in the dream the world is dreaming for us.

How's That Old Complaint?

When Daniel Webster wanted to give a person the impression that he remembered him, but could not recall his name or where they had met before, he would ask: "How's that old complaint?" Nine times out of ten the person would begin to unfold some grievance that he had discussed on a former occasion, and thereby identify himself.

- As long as we think of ourselves as bodies, we will experience ourselves as victims.
- We will also experience ourselves as lonely and deprived.
- When we see ourselves as victims then we must think that someone is after us.
- Perceiving ourselves as attacked, we are attacked.
- It is therefore a natural defense to attack back.

In the thinking of the world, nothing justifies attack more than being attacked. In truth, whenever we attack error in another we hurt ourselves. We cannot know our brothers and sisters when we attack them. No matter how much we may call someone a friend whenever we attack we make our friend a stranger (T- 3. III. 7:1-3). Following the laws of the ego we can justify attack, but we attack only ourselves. In the same way, whenever we forgive, we forgive only ourselves. The problem never did lie with the other person, whom I failed to recognize as my savior.

By its very nature the experience of deprivation breeds attack. To feel deprived we must feel *something has been or is being taken away from us.* It might be an inheritance, a degree, a promotion at work or rank in office. Or we might say of ourselves that we were deprived of a proper childhood.

According to the laws of the ego:
- If I do not have enough it must be your fault.
- You deprived me of something,
- You took something away from me.
- I am insufficient.
- You are a thief because you took my happiness from me.

Our experience of deprivation justifies our attack. As long as we believe in deprivation, attack will be perceived as our road to salvation.

Sin Demands a Victim

When things go wrong someone must be responsible. It must be you. Jesus' teaching did not conform to the tradition of the day. He had not been a good boy. He spoke with blasphemy, saying: "I and the Father are one." This indignity could not go unpunished. But, we cannot make an example of someone and not make an example of ourselves. What we define and identify as real we make real. We cannot seek out sin, provide testimony to its reality and then try to overlook it. The fact that we make it real means we cannot overlook it.

> Only my condemnation injures me.
> Only Forgiveness sets me free.
> W-pl. 198.9:3&4

Fearful Dreaming and Suffering

Suffering is a statement to the world about how bad the world has been to us. The word *suffer* comes from Latin and means *to carry* or *to bear*. As long as we live with illusions, we will not understand why misfortune seems to fall upon us. Not understanding what has befallen us, we can wail and moan and tell the world how unjustly we have been treated. The Holy Spirit needs happy learners; and as long as we wallow in misery, we are not going to be able to learn the lesson which He has set before us (T-14. II. 4:5).

Nighttime dreams are quite ego oriented. Notice how many dreams involve running or flying or trying to get away from some pursuer. Or we may dream that something is about to be found out about us that we do not want others to know. In such dreams do we not see ourselves as victims? You are being pursued. Someone is after you. Therefore, you have a right to be paranoid, don't you?

Goldstein goes to a psychiatrist. He says, "Doc, I have this terrible feeling that everybody's trying to take advantage of me."

The psychiatrist says, "Relax, Mr. Goldstein. It's a common thing. Everybody thinks that people are trying to take advantage of them."

Goldstein says, "Doc, that's such a relief. How much do I owe you?"

The psychiatrist says: "How much have you got?"

When we are victims, *all we know is what has been done to us* and we probably spend a good deal of our time telling the world exactly how unfairly we have been treated. When we are victims we are convinced that our problems came to us from the outside. We are not ourselves the cause of our suffering, someone else is. If the source of our suffering is coming from outside then we can claim that we are not responsible for our suffering. According to the ego:

> The *reasoning* by which the world is made,
> on which it rests, by which it is maintained,
> is simply this: *You* are the cause of what I do.
> Your presence justifies my wrath,
> and you exist and think apart from me.
> While you attack I must be innocent.
> And what I suffer from is your attack.
> No one who looks upon this *reasoning* exactly as it is
> could fail to see it does not follow and it makes no sense.
> Yet it seems sensible,
> because it looks as if the world were hurting you.
> T- 27. VII. 3:1-6

The Escape from Victimhood

Is there, then, no way out of this unhappy state? The Course says that there is. What is required is that we stop living according to the laws of the ego and start living according to the laws of God.

> There is a way of finding certainty right here and now.
> Refuse to be a part of fearful dreams whatever form they take,
> for you will lose identity in them.
> T- 28. IV. 2:1&2

This is a very clear declarative statement from Jesus.

Refuse to be a part of fearful dreams whatever form they take. There is a way of being happy right here and right now. All we have to do is:

- refuse to be a part of fearful dreaming.
  It's that simple.
- Give up the idea of victimhood.
- Give up our fearful projections.

84

This requires being responsible for the way we see everything. It requires our forgiveness of everything. It requires our love.

We are thus well advised not to think or speak ill of anyone else for any reason. Not only does all of our behavior have its consequence, so does all of our thinking. Some may reason that it does not hurt to think ill of someone as long as we don't attack them in any way. The Course takes this a step further and says that all of our thoughts have their consequence, whether we act on them or not. The trick is in not thinking it, but we can begin by holding our tongue. Catch yourself and stop it before the illusion takes over.

> *The boneless tongue, so small and weak,*
> *can crush and kill*, declares the Greek.
> *The tongue destroys a greater hoard,*
> the Turk asserts, *than does the sword.*
> The Persian proverb wisely saith,
> *A lengthy tongue—an early death!*
> Or sometimes takes this form instead,
> *Don't let your tongue cut off your head.*
> *The tongue can speak with such speed,*
> say the Chinese, *it outstrips the steed.*
> The Arab sages said in part,
> *The tongue's great storehouse is the heart.*
> From Hebrew was the maxim sprung,
> *Thy feet should slip, but ne'er thy tongue.*
> The sacred writer crowns the whole,
> *Who keeps thy tongue, doth keep his soul.*
> Source unknown

Condemn and *we are made prisoners.* Forgive and *we are set free* (T-27. VIII. 13:1). We are at all times prisoners to our own thoughts. Muck about in gossip, rumors and lies, and we entrap ourselves. Forgiveness is the only road that leads out of disaster, suffering and victimhood.

> The mind is in its own place
> and can make a hell out of heaven or a heaven out of hell.
> John Milton

85

Only the ego lives in isolation; only the ego thinks of itself as deprived. When we know who we are—when we recognize our identity as a Son of God—then we know we can be lacking in nothing. Everything we need has already been given to us. In the first place we have our mind. A sane mind is a thing of great joy. It is the essence of us. I read *No Matter Where You Go, There You Are* by Jon Cabot Zinn, a seasoned meditator and teacher of Zen Buddhism. And what is the conclusion he comes to in his book? Simply this—as the hero in the movie Buckaroo Bonsai says: "No matter where you go, there you are." It's all in the mind. It's all a decision, a choice about how we want to see things. What do you want to see?

Extension, the Right Form of Projection
Just as there is a correct form of denial—namely the denial of error—so too is there a right-minded attitude.

We have learned, however, that there *is* an alternative to projection.
Every ability of the ego has a better use,
because its abilities are directed by the mind,
which has a better Voice.
The Holy Spirit extends and the ego projects.
As their goals are opposed, so is the result.
T-6. II. 4:1-4

We can extend love or fear, comfort or pain. With the Holy Spirit we can see the world and ourselves as whole, healthy and worthy of love. When we judge another, we do not know what circumstances stand behind their behavior. We cannot be intolerant and happy at the same time. Our intolerance keeps us from our own happiness. We experience true happiness to the degree to which we can learn to leave things alone without thinking that we need to change them.

Projecting doesn't work. It doesn't get us what we want. It doesn't satisfy. It doesn't bring happiness. As we judge so are we judged. Forgive and we are set free. It's a law, a simple basic law of spirit.

Chapter 8

The Law of Gentleness

Then the King will say to those at his right hand,
    "Come, O blessed of my Father, inherit the kingdom
    prepared for you from the foundation of the world;
for I was hungry and you gave me food,
    I was thirsty and you gave me drink,
    I was a stranger and you welcomed me,
I was naked and you clothed me,
    I was sick and you visited me,
    I was in prison and you came to me."
Then the righteous will answer him,
    "Lord, when did we see thee hungry and feed thee,
    or thirsty and give thee drink?
And when did we see thee a stranger and welcome thee,
    naked and clothe thee?
And when did we see thee sick or in prison
    and visit thee?"
And the King will answer them, "Truly, I say to you,
    as you did it to one of the least of these my brethren,
    you did it to me."
                  Matthew 25:34-40

A kind heart is a fountain of gladness,
making everything in its vicinity freshen into smiles.
                  Washington Irving

The fourth characteristic of a teacher of God is gentleness. Though the word is *gentleness* the Course also uses the words *kindness* and *gentleness* interchangeably. From the beginning of the section on gentleness we read:

Harm is impossible for God's teachers.
They can neither harm nor be harmed.
Harm is the outcome of judgment.

It is the dishonest act that follows a dishonest thought.
It is a verdict of guilt upon a brother,
and therefore on oneself.
It is the end of peace and the denial of learning.
M-4. IV. 1:1-6

As our purpose is undoing, or removing, the blocks to an awareness of love's presence, the section on gentleness begins by talking about harm, its very opposite. It is harm, the wish to judge, our lack of tolerance and open-mindedness that lead to anger and attack. Gentleness comes about as we *let go of our inclination to harm.* In the eyes of the world Jesus was harmed on the cross. The traditional Christian perspective is that he suffered, bled and died *for our sins.* According to the Course, Jesus knew he was not a body and therefore did not suffer, though by the definitions of this world his body may have been harmed. Only a mind can be sick and suffer. Jesus knew who he was and was not caught in fear; therefore he did not suffer. God cannot suffer.

To Attack and to Confront

The law of gentleness relates back to our second law of honesty, as harm is a *dishonest thought.* The dishonest thought is that it is actually possible to be separated from God. Attack is obviously a form of disunity. Attack never works. This is not to say that we should never disagree with someone. The trick is in the ability to disagree without attack—without anger. Anger keeps the ego alive but anger begins to disappear when we realize that we have no need of it. In short, it never helps us.

Therefore, God's teachers are wholly gentle.
They need the strength of gentleness,
for it is in this that the function of salvation becomes easy.
M - 4. IV. 2:1

My experience of Ken Wapnick is that he has always been wholly gentle with me even while disagreeing with me. It takes skill to teach without attack. It takes skill to be a parent or schoolteacher who can confront without anger, attack, spite or malice. Good teachers never terrorize their students (T-3.I.4:5). Ken Wapnick writes in *A Course in Miracles and Christianity*: "I have frequently

88

made the public comment that one of the most important lessons a student of *A Course in Miracles* can learn is how to disagree with someone (whether that person be on another spiritual path, or a student of the Course) without it being an attack." (Page 4.) Disagreement without attack is only possible if we have no investment in how the other person is supposed to respond.

Jesus says in the Gospels that he is gentle and humble in heart and for this reason his yoke is easy and his burden light. He could say that because he was not himself caught up in ego problems. He did not suffer any stress regardless of what was happening.

> The might of God's teachers lies in their gentleness,
> for they have understood their evil thoughts
> came neither from God's Son nor his Creator.
> M-4. IV. 2:8

Kindness—Dealing with Each Other

When you notice the way we deal with other people, it becomes obvious that there are a number of tactics that are helpful in promoting peace and goodwill. There are also a number of attitudes and actions that we may think are helpful but repeatedly produce negative rather than positive results and ultimately prove debilitating rather than helpful.

The attitude with which we approach the world determines the world we see, and the world we see is the world we receive. A gentle mind sees a world of gentleness (W-pII. 8.3:5). A hostile mind sees a world of hostility. We can see holiness and hope—or we can see sickness, sadness, catastrophe and disaster. Regardless of whatever happens, we are never wrong in following the law of gentleness.

One of the primary characteristics of Jesus is his gentleness. The historical Jesus was kind to the poor, the sick, to children, to prostitutes, to tax collectors, to his accusers, and those who tried and crucified him. He was kind to the soldiers who stood at the foot of his cross and jeered at him and to the thief who died with him on the cross.

What is the first quality we think of when we think of someone like Mother Theresa, Gandhi or Martin Luther King Jr.? Is it not their gentleness? One of the best examples we have of gentleness is St. Francis of Assisi. St. Francis regarded everything as his brother and his sister—thus the title of the movie made about his life, *Brother Sun, Sister Moon*. All animals, trees and flowers were friends to St. Francis. His gentleness extended so deeply that when his robe once caught fire, and one of his brothers ran to put it out, he is reported to have said: "Don't hurt Brother Fire." Why, with these examples before us, would we ever want to make others feel guilty for what *we think* they did to us?

When kindness has left people even for a few moments,
we become afraid of them, as if their reason had left them.
Willa Cather: *My Mortal Enemy*

When we are cruel rather than gentle, our reason—or our right mind—has left us. We are now living according to the laws of the ego rather than the laws of Spirit. Students of the Course thus come to know that whenever they are angry, upset, disturbed, perturbed, envious, jealous, or projecting in any way, they simply are not in their right mind. Therefore, another way of looking at the world is called for. In such a moment a better, clearer pathway is both needed and possible.

Kindness is a language which the dumb can speak
and the deaf can hear and understand.
Christian Nestell Bovee

If you are training an animal and you want to get the animal to do things in accordance with your wishes, the best way to do it is with gentleness. When we treat animals with kindness, they trust us and willingly share their lives with us. There is a wonderful story about a prison where they allowed the prisoners to have pets. There was one man on death row who was given a kitten. He loved and cared for that kitten with tremendous gentleness and all because he said, "It was the only thing that had ever loved me."

The inclination to goodness
is imprinted deeply in the nature of man;

in so much that if it issues not toward men
it will take on to other living creatures.
Francis Bacon

When someone is sick we usually treat them with gentleness.
When people are old and crippled, we treat them with gentleness. If
gentleness is the best way to deal with animals, the dumb, the deaf,
the lame, the blind, the old and the sick—why should we think that
living according to ego laws is going to help us?

In the middle of my near-death experience, I saw that love
was the only way out. I found the door only when I stopped trying to
manipulate and control. When I finally relinquished all power, I
gained some control. I was here and I understood that I had a great
deal to be thankful for in just being alive. I further understood that
the best way to treat my brothers and sisters was with kindness.
Those who have near-death experiences inevitably come back and
say they now understand that the only thing to do is to love. It is the
only reason any of us are here.

The Key Marked Gentleness

No matter how confused we are—no matter how upset or
how much we may think the world has mistreated us—there is
always an exit. There is a simple law we can follow. It is the law of
gentleness. It may go by other names such as kindness, courtesy,
altruism, charity, mercy, grace, hospitality or accommodation. It is
all simply gentleness. Start with the key marked "gentleness" and we
can open all doors that lead to love. Love is home. Home is the place
every pilgrim wants to be. Eventually, the path of destiny leads us
home. We may get confused in this journey—there are many things
to pull us off track—but getting back on track is simple. It just
requires the application of one simple law of happiness, the law that
says: *gentleness will always work.* In fact it can work miracles.

God in the Course is spoken of as "the maker of the world of
gentleness" (T-25. III. 8:1). Workbook lesson 222 reads: God is with
me. I live and move in Him. One line from that lesson reads: *He
covers me with kindness and with care, and holds in love the Son He
shines upon, who also shines on Him.* (W-pII. 222. 1:4). Forgiveness

91

is a demonstration of gentleness. In *The Song of Prayer* it speaks of *forgiveness' kindness.* (S-2.I.1:4). To forgive is a kind thing to do.

Practicing Gentleness

Gentleness is a simple thing. It is not hard to practice. There are many ways to exercise our gentleness and we can practice it every moment of every day. Just as we would be gentle with animals, or with the crippled, we can apply it to the customer who just took advantage of our generosity, the gas station attendant, the doorman, the taxi cab driver, the harried waitress, the seemingly thoughtless driver ahead of us on the road. Be aware and recognize things that others miss. Be gentle with the harassed sales clerk. With Sarah I must constantly practice nonjudgmental gentleness. She wants nothing less from me and we are both happier because of it.

Gentleness is the beginning and the end of the law.
Ancient Hebrew Proverb

When I perform funerals and interview relatives before the service to gather information for a eulogy, I notice that the first, most positive and powerful thing anyone can say about another human being after they are dead is that they were kind: to children, to animals, to everyone. What would you like to be said about you when a minister, a priest or rabbi comes to interview your family for your eulogy? Can you think of anything better than "He or she was kind or gentle?" Think of the best moments in your own life. It was probably when you were being kind to someone else, or when you experienced someone being kind to you. If we can cultivate gentleness within ourselves gentleness will cultivate us.

No matter how dark another heart may *seem* to be, someplace deep inside there is a *Real Self*, a gentle, kind being seeking to get out. The best way to help them get out is to practice a little gentleness. Gentleness is always an appropriate response and the moment is always now. We cannot do good to another and not also benefit ourselves.

It is one of the beautiful compensations of life that no one can sincerely try to help another without helping himself.
Charles Dudley Warner

92

Gentleness to Oneself

We need to be kind to ourselves in keeping with the law that says as we give so do we receive. There is a section in *The Song of Prayer* entitled "Forgiveness of Yourself," which talks about true forgiveness. We don't understand forgiveness until we've forgiven ourselves. To forgive ourselves is an act of kindness. It means allowing ourselves the joy and privilege of being able to listen to the Voice for God instead of placing ourselves under the tyrannical laws of the ego. And is it not a kindness to ourselves to hear His Voice and learn the simple lessons He would teach, instead of trying to dismiss His words, and substitute our own words in place of His (W-pI.198.5:3)?

True forgiveness asks for nothing in return. False forgiveness says: "I will forgive you on condition that you never do that again." We make attempts at kindness and forgiveness, but we get upset if people do not offer us expressions of gratitude and thanks for the good we did for them. If our gifts are not received with honor, we take them back. Yet, kindness is not a loan. We give it expecting nothing in return. We do it because it is giving to ourselves. The time to act with gentleness is now. Not for a second need we wait. Now is the opportunity. Now is the time.

> You cannot do a kindness too soon,
> for you never know how soon it will be too late.
> Ralph Waldo Emerson

Be kind and gentle and make it complete. Make it full. Make it whole. Make it now. When I was eighteen years old I read the following passage in a book. I liked it so much I cut it out of the book and pasted it on the mirror in my bedroom. It reads:

> I expect to pass through this life but once,
> If, therefore, there be any kindness I can show
> or any good thing I can do to any fellow being, let me do it now.
> Let me not defer nor neglect it, for I shall not pass this way again.
> William Penn

> My religion is simple. My religion is kindness.
> Dalai Lama

Spread love everywhere you go.
Let no one ever come to you without leaving better and happier.
Be the living expression of God's kindness:
kindness in your face, kindness in your eyes, kindness in your smile,
kindness in your warm greeting.
Mother Theresa

Gentleness is so big, so beyond us, so powerful, that it is *greater than all wisdom of the wise.* It is greater because it works. It is the way God works in relationship to us.

It is wiser to be kind than to be wise.
Noah ben Shea

Lesson 67 from the Workbook is: *Love created me like itself.* Take a moment to repeat for yourself these four lines from Lesson 67.

Holiness created me holy.
Kindness created me kind.
Helpfulness created me helpful.
Perfection created me perfect.
W-pI.67.2:3-6

Chapter 9

The Law of Joy

Joy is the inevitable result of gentleness.
Gentleness means that fear is now impossible,
and what could come to interfere with joy?
The open hands of gentleness are always filled.
The gentle have no pain. They cannot suffer.
Why would they not be joyous?
M-4. V. 1:1-6

What Is Joy?
The fifth characteristic of a teacher of God is joy. Joy, however, is more of a consequence, more of an effect than a cause.

One day I was driving in a city in Florida I had never been in before. I got into the left lane of a three-lane highway. At a stop light I suddenly realized that I was not in the center lane but a left turning lane. There was little traffic around at the time, so when the light changed I tried to go straight ahead instead of turning left. Some man to my right started honking his horn at me, rolled down his window, and started screaming obscenities in my direction, letting me know exactly what an idiot I was. Indeed, I had made a mistake and gotten into the wrong lane of traffic, so some reaction was not surprising. However, as we proceeded down the street, he got in front of me and began driving slowly so that I also had to drive slowly, and so did everyone behind us. He now proceeded to give me the finger. As he seemed inclined to keep this up, I made a left turn behind him just to get away from him.

According to the chaotic laws of the ego, if you anger, frustrate or upset me, I am entitled to get angry and have the right to frustrate or upset you. Did the fellow in front of me really enjoy trying to annoy me and others because I was in a state of lost-lane confusion?

Lesson 68 from the Workbook says:
Miracles hold no grievances.
We cannot hold a grievance and know ourselves. The Holy Spirit sees everything as either an expression of love or a call for love. When we see only love—all we know is love. There is simply no room for any grievance and in this there is great joy.

The Course is trying to teach us to associate misery with the ego and joy with the spirit (T-4.IV.5:6). Only Spirit is truly joyful. We have, however, taught ourselves that joy is of the ego and misery is of the spirit. Doing what we might think of as "spiritual things" (being nice to other people, meditating, praying, going to church, and being generous) may not sound like much fun. Joy from the ego's point of view is *getting what we think we want.* On an ego level, however, we do not know what we want, only what we do not want.

The principle of Atonement and the separation
began at the same time.
When the ego was made, God placed in the mind the call to joy.
This call is so strong that the ego always dissolves at its sound.
T-5. II. 3:1-3

We must choose to hear one of two voices. One we made ourselves. The other has been given to us by God. The Holy Spirit is in us in a very literal sense. All we have to do is pay attention to the call. The Holy Spirit is calling us back to the place where we have always been and will forever be (T- 5. II. 3:4-8).

Looking for the Inside on the Outside
Joy comes through the denial of the negative. It does not involve the destruction of the ego because the ego, being nothing, does not need to be destroyed. To be joyful all we need to do is to stop confirming an illusion. Joy comes in the happy recognition of what is truly valuable. Joy comes in the affirmation of spirit and the denial of the power of the ego to rule over us.

Someone once said, *No one can ever get too much of what they don't need.* It is perhaps no surprise that the ego looks for a quick fix, an easy solution, a shot, a relief. Depression comes from a sense of being deprived; but we cannot feel deprived of anything

96

unless we first decide that something outside of us will make us happy (T-4. IV. 3:2&3). Where do we look for a confirmation of reality? Ego looks without and Spirit looks within. The highest suicide rates in the United States are in those cities which permit gambling. Though we are all invested in form—form is never enough. It's not the exterior (exoteric) but the interior (esoteric) that holds the meaning of life.

I read an article about a study on happiness that had been done by a group of social psychologists. Their conclusion: *there is no one thing that can be said to make us happy.* Happiness is subjective. Nevertheless, the study did find some basic traits that lead to happiness. What made for happiness was not *success, youth, good looks, money or any of those sometimes envied assets.* The clear winner was *close relationships.* The study said *supportive, intimate connections with other people* was *the most important ingredient in being happy.* The thing that makes us happy is the experience of *loving* and *being loved.* The study concluded that the most unhappy people were those who were not experiencing the give and take of loving relationships.

Joy Comes in Sharing

Grief can take care of itself, but to get the full value of joy,
you must have somebody to divide it with.
Mark Twain

As an author and lecturer I travel a great deal. Whenever I get to a beautiful setting, like the mountains and lakes of Idaho or perhaps a beach at midnight, my first thought is always, "I wish Dolores and Sarah were with me." Ultimately, we cannot find joy for ourselves alone anymore than we can pray for ourselves alone. We cannot hear the Voice for God in ourselves alone because we are not alone (T-9.II. 6:1).

The law of joy, like the law of honesty, comes with the denial of the false and the affirmation of the truth. Joy is the result of no longer holding on to guilt. Joy comes in no longer needing to hide. What could be more joyful than to acknowledge the truth and have it be wholly wonderful? When we are willing to hide nothing, we also experience peace and joy (T-1. IV.1:5).

Joy and Freedom

One summer I decided to take a wilderness survival training course. Along with a group of new acquaintances from New York City, I drove my Volkswagen camper up into the Adirondack Mountains in upstate New York where we joined a few others in a seven-day training program, followed by each of us being alone in the woods for three days. The program was educational and fun. We learned how to climb cliffs and live off the land, and we enjoyed socializing with each other.

There was one problem, however. We had two trainers, a young man and a young woman. I remember very little about the man but the woman left an impression on all of us. She seemed out to prove herself and laid down the law like a drill sergeant. Everyone was very stoic about this and very polite; no one said anything to her about her bossy, arrogant manner. For some reason we also never talked to each other about her. On the day we left, however, as we pulled out of the parking lot and onto the main road, everyone in the van burst out laughing. For the next several minutes we were in an uproar. No one had to say anything about why. We all knew we were laughing because we were free of her tyranny. What had happened? Our new freedom had brought us joy. Think about when you have felt real joy in your life and I'll bet it was when you felt free. Joy comes to us when an insight dawns in the mind. Joy comes with waking up. Revelation is a waking up, it is a rebirth.

> Miracles are a way of earning release from fear.
> Revelation induces a state
> in which fear has already been abolished.
> Miracles are thus a means and revelation is an end.
> T-1. I. 28

Joy comes with release. Joy comes when a burden has been lifted from us. Jesus carried no burdens, thus he could say:

> Come to me, all you who labor and are heavy laden
> and I will give you rest.

Take my yoke upon you and learn from me,
for I am gentle and humble in heart,
and you will find rest for your souls.
For my yoke is easy and my burden is light.
Matthew 11: 28-30

That could only be said by someone who is free and unburdened. Jesus had nothing to carry around with him, no burdens to place upon us. Joy comes in revelation. Joy comes when the burden of guilt is lifted from us. It comes when we are healed. It comes when we know we are forgiven. Joy comes in freshness. Joy comes with that which is new. Nothing beats a new love. And there is no reason why our present love cannot forever become new. Someone once said that: "There is more in the other than you will ever get to know." We never get to know each other completely when all we have is our rational minds. We're never going to figure it all out. Revelation comes not as the result of figuring things out. We come to the truth, not through knowledge but through experience. Joy comes in opening one's heart so there can be even more love. Love is endless and so is joy.

True joy is something which happens inside the mind. Joy comes in no longer living according to the laws of the ego. To be joyful is to be free and to extend freedom. It means holding on to nothing. Joy would place upon our brothers no restrictions. Joy is a free expression. There is no freedom as wonderful as freedom from guilt and fear. Freedom from guilt comes in knowing the truth. Knowing the truth dispels illusion. Joy has within it no attack thoughts. If there is no attack—there is no guilt. Freedom from guilt is pure joy—true joy. The truth is joyful because it is a freeing experience.

There is a wonderful story told about Dr. William Thetford, Dr. Helen Schucman's collaborator in putting together *A Course in Miracles*. On the night of July 3rd, 1988, Bill was visiting with Judy Skutch Whitson. That evening he was unusually exuberant and he announced: "I'm flexible. I'm finally flexible. I'm not rigid any more." He extended his arms and danced around the room and he kept saying: "I'm free. All my relationships feel so wonderfully peaceful and free." The next morning after breakfast and meditation

99

Bill set out for a walk. Then, his heart stopped. Bill, like Thomas Jefferson and John Adams, chose July 4 as the day he left this world. Death at the proper, chosen moment must be a blissful experience.

Pain and Pleasure

Think of pleasure and you may think of good food, good drink, a good back rub, or good sex. You might think of something thrilling, a ride at a carnival, skiing, swimming. All these pleasures are associated with the body and all are at best fleeting—temporary. Satisfy a hunger and you will soon be hungry again. I'm not saying our eyes should not delight in a beautiful sunset, or that we should not enjoy good food or love making. But all such experiences are temporary. Joy comes not in the temporal but the eternal. It comes in knowing who we really are. The body is not evil. It is not good, it is not bad. It is totally neutral. Like the ego, it is part of an illusion, something which is itself not eternal. Nothing which turns to dust is eternal. Only the eternal is forever true. Only in the truth is there joy.

If we are honest with ourselves, we all know it's never really about the external. Sex is never just about sex, it's about the relationship. The relationship is the important thing. And what is the relationship about? It's about trust and honesty and tolerance and patience and all those things that lead to true happiness.

Pain demonstrates the body must be real.
It is a loud, obscuring voice
whose shrieks would silence what the Holy Spirit says,
and keep His words from your awareness.
T-27. VI. 1:1&2

Pain is a great and annoying distraction, that takes our peace away. Pain and pleasure both confirm the reality of the body. Yet, physical pain and pleasure are equally unreal (T- 27. VII. 1:1-8).

God's Witness sees no witnesses against the body.
Neither does He harken to the witnesses by other names
that speak in other ways for its reality. He knows it is not real.
Its pains and pleasures does He heal alike,
for all sin's witnesses does His replace.
T- 27. VI. 4:1-3 & 9

100

The Confusion of Joy and Pain

The *body* is neutral, as is every *thing*. Only the mind makes anything real. It is true in the world of the ego. It is true in the world of God. On an ego level our most obvious reality is a body. The body is the ego's chosen home (T. 23. I. 3:3) and we give reality to our bodies through pleasures and pains, through a hundred forms that surround and distract us. Yet the body does not make us real. Nor does the body give us joy.

> Pain is illusion; joy reality.
> Pain is but sleep; joy is awaking.
> Pain is deception; joy alone is truth.
> W-pI.190. 10:4-6

The Holy Spirit teaches us how to tell the difference between joy and pain. The confusion of joy and pain is the cause of the idea of sacrifice. To the traditional Christian it looks as though Jesus had to give up his body and suffer upon a cross as a payment for sin. There is no joy in suffering. There is no joy in the cross. Joy is found only in the resurrection. Joy comes in freedom from suffering.

Only spirit can know pure joy. Joy comes in letting go of all that which would hurt and harm us. It comes in the release from all guilt and fear. It is knowing that one is a child of God, a wonderful, blessed, eternal child. Our future can only get better as we grow in this awareness. Not having our own agenda, carrying with us no preconceptions about the way things are supposed to be, life can be wonderfully joyful and freeing. Joy comes in being free and released from pain. Joy comes in knowing our reality as His Sons and Daughters.

> We are free in that moment when we let go to God.
> All we have to do is make a commitment.
> All we have to do is tell the truth.
> All we have to do is trust in God.

Joy comes in doing His will and living according to His laws. It is the joyous discovery that His Voice is our Voice and we are all one with God. The ego is so ready to attack, so ready to jump to the

defense, so ready to find something wrong. Spirit only blesses the
world.

The constancy of joy
is a condition quite alien to your understanding.
Yet if you could even imagine what it must be,
you would desire it although you understand it not.
The constancy of happiness has no exceptions;
no change of any kind.
. . .
Reason will tell you that you cannot ask for happiness inconstantly.
For if what you desire you receive, and happiness is constant,
then you need ask for it but once to have it always.
T-21. VIII.2:1-3 & 3:1&2

She gives most who gives with joy.
The best way to show our gratitude to God
and His people is to accept everything with joy.
A joyful heart is the inevitable result
of a heart burning with love.
Never let anything so fill you with sorrow
as to make you forget the joy of the Christ risen.
Mother Theresa

Joy is prayer. Joy is strength. Joy is love.

Chapter 10

The Law of Defenselessness

The sixth characteristic of a teacher of God is defenselessness.

One evening Dolores and I sat down to watch television. First we watched the "Biography" show on the life of mobster John Gotti. That was followed by "Eye to Eye" with Connie Chung, about the growing disrespect, insolence, impudence, impertinence, and profanity that characterize American society. This is true, the show said, in schools, in the workplace and in the home. It pointed to the proliferation of muckraking on a number of daytime talk shows and in the tabloids and the long list of murders and acts of violence that daily fill our newspapers and newscasts. That show was followed by a 20/20 documentary on the violent behavior of children.

The next morning I read an article in *Reader's Digest* entitled "What Happened to Civility?" by Richard Bookhiser. The article began: "America has become a rude country. Drivers cut across lanes of traffic as if the turn-signal had never been invented. Businesses put callers on hold, forcing us to listen to annoying music. People push in and out of elevators like hockey players facing off over a puck. . . ."

The next evening we watched a documentary on road rage. Watching these documentaries and reading an article about rudeness and duress, I got to thinking about a line from the movie *Grand Canyon* in which the character played by Danny Glover turns to a group of thugs who are about to beat up Kevin Kline and says: "You know, it's not supposed to be this way."

If it is true that things are getting worse, then we need to change things. What we need to change is not the world or other people. What we have to change is ourselves. The Course is here to

103

help us experience a turnaround in consciousness so that we can look at things differently. The ego's natural response is to be on the defensive, to do whatever it can to protect itself from perceived attack. As long as we are on the defensive, there is not much of a chance we will change anything.

We need to do a "180" and look at things in a wholly new way without the defensiveness which so often characterizes this world. We need a willingness to look at ourselves and recognize our own responsibility in what is going on without the constant need for projection. When faced with attack, criticism and condemnation, it is helpful to recognize these six possibilities:

1. Safety Lies in Defenselessness
We are so well defended and we jump to the defense with such ease we don't take the time to ask what it is that we are defending and why. What are we defending, a frail little ego, an illusion, a dream?

No one can become an advanced teacher of God until he
fully understands that defenses are but
foolish guardians of mad illusions.
The more grotesque the dream,
the fiercer and more powerful its defenses seem to be.
It is not danger that comes when defenses are laid down.
It is safety. It is peace. It is joy. And it is God.
M-4.VI. 1:6&7 & 11-15

The defenses the ego sets up are indeed mad illusions, and the more grotesque the dream, the fiercer and more powerful the defense. Mob boss John Gotti had a son who was run over and killed when he rode his bicycle out between two cars into the path of an oncoming car. The family was outraged. The man who accidentally killed Gotti's son was later literally chopped into pieces. Although it was an accident, Gotti felt it necessary to physically annihilate the man who killed his son.

Jesus on the cross is showing us that ultimately we must be defenseless. It is true on a soul level. It is true on all levels. Ultimately, we stand naked before God. There is no effective attack,

104

blame or defense to be offered before God against any person. Excuses don't work in Heaven and they don't work here, either.

Defenselessness is all that is required
for the truth to dawn upon our minds with certainty.
W-pI. 135. 21:3

Defenselessness relates back to our second law of honesty, as we need to be totally defenseless before truth can enter into our mind. In my near-death experience I was, on an ego level, annihilated and devastated. There was no excuse, no apology, no defense of self that would work in front of what loomed large before me. As long as we defend we cannot know the truth, for what we are defending is not true. God needs no defense. Only the ego thinks it needs a defense.

Defenselessness is strength.
W-pI. 153. 6:1

Defenselessness can never be attacked,
because it recognizes a strength so great attack is folly.
W-pI. 153. 6:4

To speak of a law of defenselessness doesn't mean we should not protect our body if someone physically attacks us. Defenselessness does not mean permitting destructive behavior, letting others take advantage of us, or living under conditions we find unbearable.

2. All Attack Is a Call for Help

Even if we think someone mistreated us, rather than jumping to the defense before we think about what we are doing, can we not realize that they acted out of fear and ignorance? Can we not see mistakes as a call for help? *Forgiveness is the natural reaction to distress that rests on error, and thus calls for help.* Forgiveness is, after all, the only sane response (T-30. VI. 2:7).

During the Korean War, a South Korean civilian was arrested by the communists and ordered shot. When the young communist leader learned that the prisoner was in charge of an orphanage, caring for small children, he decided to spare him and kill the man's son instead. So they shot the man's nineteen-year-old boy in the presence of his father. Later the fortunes of war changed, and the young communist leader was captured by the United Nations forces, tried and condemned to death. Before the sentence could be carried out, the South Korean whose son had been killed pleaded for the life of the communist, saying: "He was young, he did not know what he was doing." The United Nations forces granted his request, and the father took the murderer of his son into his own home.

Jesus from the cross says: "Father, forgive them for they know not what they do." He did not say that so God would know what to do. He said it so *we* would know what to do in much less severe circumstances. When someone is going crazy in our presence, they really do not know what they are doing. If they do not know what they are doing they need our help, not our attack.

3. In the Presence of Attack, Criticism and Condemnation Ask: Is This Something I Would Accuse Myself of Doing?

Lesson 134 from the Workbook suggests that when we are tempted to accuse someone of sin in any form, we should not allow our mind to dwell on what we think he did. We should ask instead: *Would I accuse myself of doing this* (W-pI. 134. 9:2&3)?

> Who would send messages of hatred and attack
> if he but understood he sends them to himself?
> Who would accuse, make guilty and condemn himself?
> T-19. IV. (B) 14:11

In the story of the woman caught in adultery, Jesus says that the one who is without sin should cast the first stone. Beginning with the eldest, they drop their stones and walk away. Jesus then turns to the woman and says, "Woman, where are your accusers?" To which she says, "Lord, there are none." Jesus then replies, "Neither do I condemn you, go and sin no more." *To accuse is not to understand* (T-14. V. 3:6).

We have all been gluttons, selfish, egocentric and self-absorbed. We have all condemned others, in our minds if nowhere else. Since we did all these things, it is helpful to ask ourselves if this is something we would accuse ourselves of doing? An old plaque I found in an antique store says:

> There is so much bad in the best of us
> And so much good in the worst of us
> That it hardly behooves any of us
> To talk about the rest of us.

4. What Lesson Can I Learn in This Experience?
Reversing the Laws of the Ego

When we have difficulty with our brothers or sisters, it is helpful to listen carefully to the criticism they offer and suspend our defensiveness long enough to allow ourselves the opportunity to see things differently. Whenever anyone has any criticism of us for even the smallest thing, rather than jumping to the defense, which is what the ego is most inclined to do, we can listen carefully and ask ourselves:

1. Why is this person saying what they are saying?
2. Is there even a grain of truth in what they are saying?
3. Is there some way I might change to make things better?

Remember, the ego always speaks first (T-5. VI. 3:5 & T-6. IV.1:2). Lesson 6 says "I am never upset for the reason I think." Therefore, whether my brother is "wrong" or "right" I have to ask the question, "Why am I upset?" Here is a real opportunity for insight. This is the deeper meaning of doing unto others as we would have them do unto us. Is there a *glimmer of truth* in the lesson my brother would have me learn? Do I believe any of this is real?

5. Teach No One He Has Hurt You

Everyone to whom we offer healing returns it, because we offer it to ourselves. Everyone we attack keeps the attack and holds it against us. God is the only Cause and God does not cause guilt. What is not of God cannot have power over us. We should teach no one that he has hurt us, for if we do, we teach ourselves that what is not of God has power over us. We should therefore teach no one that he is what we would not want to be (T-7. VII.3:8). We would never attack another unless we believed that he had somehow taken the peace of God from us. No one, however, can take the peace of God

107

from us. If we give another the power to take the peace of God from us, it is we who gave them that power.

6. Forgiveness Must Be Total

Then Peter went up to him and said,
Lord, how often must I forgive my brother
if he wrongs me? As often as seven times?
Jesus answered,
Not seven, I tell you, but seventy times seven.
Matthew 8:21-22

There is no order of difficulty in miracles. We cannot forgive some people but not others. There cannot be some things we forgive in someone but other things about that same person we cannot forgive. There cannot then be some forms of guilt that we cannot forgive (T-30.VI.7:7). Forgiveness is not something we do sometimes. To forgive seventy times seven means to forgive repeatedly, no matter how wrong we might think another has been, no matter how many times we may *think* we have been abused. The answer remains: *Forgive. Forgive. Forgive. Let it go. Let it go. Let it go.*

Aggression never succeeds. Jesus on the cross was denied and betrayed even by Peter. If there was ever someone who *seemed* to have a right to be indignant, you might think it was Jesus. If Jesus saw sin in his disciples, if he made them wrong, if he condemned them he would be ego bound, and not the Christ.

7. Peace Is Obtainable When We Hold to These Ideas
• Peace of mind, salvation and the abundance that comes with it can be our only goal.

Forgiveness is the key to salvation and peace of mind.
Forgiveness is man's deepest need
and highest achievement.
Horace Bushnell

• Through forgiveness we see everyone, including ourselves, as guiltless. If Jesus on the cross can forgive murderers, can we not

108

be more tolerant of lesser sins which we *think* have been perpetrated against us?

• As we give up our grievances, we find ourselves becoming increasingly aware of the ever-present subtle and gentle guidance of the Holy Spirit. Following the Holy Spirit, we do not condemn others. We simply cannot.

... my judgment ... cannot be wrong because it never attacks.
T-4. IV. 10:4

It is then that we can experience peace of mind. With the Holy Spirit's guidance, it becomes possible to know what we are supposed to do and do it. When we say the Lord's Prayer we say: "Forgive us our debts *as* we forgive our debtors." As long as:

• we are unforgiving we justify the belief that whatever is wrong in the world is *outside or other than us.*
• we think there is something we cannot forgive, we block our own entrance into the Kingdom.
• we project guilt and sin upon the world we live in confusion and despair.
• we live in fear, love has no place in our hearts.

No one can take anything from us. To be alive, free and at peace—forgive.

Only as we forgive do we:
• know ourselves as God created us.
• experience Heaven.
• discover there is nothing to forgive!

Jesus assures us that as we forgive, so are we forgiven. To forgive is to overlook, to relinquish the past, to let go of everything, to hold on to nothing. In the deepest sense, *to forgive* means *to forget.* There is a saying that: *No one forgets where the hatchet is buried.* True forgiveness means there is no hatchet to bury. Let it go and go on.

As children of God, we cannot help being blessed. The essence of our being is love. It always has been so. The more innocent we are, the more we see what the Holy Spirit would have us do with our lives and the more we are able to do it.

Peace of mind occurs as we:
• drop our concern with getting.
• drop the need to be right and concentrate on giving.
• forgive.

Forgiveness is the vehicle for changing our perception and letting go of our fears, condemnations, judgments and grievances. It is helpful to give up the idea that we must defend ourselves in any way. There is nothing to forgive and nothing to defend *unless we think there is.* We're just making up the idea that there is. If we think there is something to forgive and that we need to defend then we choose to make an error real. We teach our brothers that they cannot hurt us by not making errors real.

There is nothing to hold on to—nothing !

Chapter 11

The Law of Generosity

We have said that without projection there can be no anger,
but it is also true that without extension there can be no love.
These reflect a fundamental law of the mind,
and therefore one that always operates.
It is the law by which you create and were created.
It is the law that unifies the Kingdom,
and keeps it in the Mind of God.
To the ego, the law is perceived as a means of getting rid of
something it does not want.
To the Holy Spirit, it is the fundamental law of sharing,
by which you give what you value in order to keep it in your mind.
To the Holy Spirit it is the law of extension.
To the ego it is the law of deprivation.
It therefore produces abundance or scarcity,
depending on how you choose to apply it.
This choice is up to you, but it is not up to you to decide
whether or not you will utilize the law.
Every mind must project or extend,
because that is how it lives and every mind is life.
T-7. VIII. 1:1-11

Getting to Get—Giving Away—Giving Up

The seventh characteristic of a teacher of God is generosity.
Like all the other characteristics generosity is based on trust, for
without trust no one can be truly generous. This idea does not make
any sense to the ego. To the ego, if you want to have something *you
get it—you take it* and then *it is yours.* We live in a "go for it"
society. A popular book of the early 1990s was entitled *Go For It.*
Following this line of thinking, if something is taken away from us
and we do not have it any more we feel we have been deprived.

The Law of Extension and the Law of Deprivation

There is a light that this world cannot give.
Yet you can give it, as it was given you.
And as you give it, it shines forth to call you
from the world and follow it.
For this light will attract you as nothing in this world can do.
And you will lay aside the world and find another.

T- 13. VI. 11:1-5

This world is the world as we made it. We could have made it up lots of ways. Over the vast eons of time it has been made up millions of different ways. Every age, every culture has done this. There is nothing bad about it. There is nothing good about it. It's just the way it is. Mormons hold to a formal view of the world and physical reality. They believe that those Mormons who are worthy and make it to Heaven will have bodies just as we do in this world. The Hindus and Buddhists believe in reincarnation. Catholics believe in purgatory and a yet different myth regarding Heaven and hell and the laws by which we should live.

The ego produces mythologies to define reality. The creation of a particular mythology can also be understood as excuse-making, rationalizing or justifying the reality we choose to project. Thus is mythology purely myth—that is, completely unrelated to reality. Yet at other times myths symbolically point to something deeper. From the standpoint of the Course, the Adam and Eve story in the Bible is a good way to understand how the ego came into being (mythologically). What we project or extend is real for us. This is an immutable law of the mind in this world as well as in the Kingdom (T-7.II.2:4). *"Immutable"* means constant, determinate and unalterable. According to this immutable law, *what we project is that which we believe to be true*. It doesn't mean that it is true; it's just what we believe to be true. So the question is: What is our belief and what are our projections?

We are at all times either *projecting* or *extending*. We are either projecting our interpretations and analyses upon the world or we are extending and receiving love. This basic law of the mind, which works either in the world of the ego or in the world of Spirit, produces *scarcity* or *abundance.* The more guilt we give away, the guiltier we feel. The more love we give away the more love we feel. The ego stumbles on two major drawbacks in giving its judgment to the world.

1. Conflict cannot be shared because it separates. While we may attempt to share conflict, no one wants to be the recipient of conflict. Wishing for conflict is a wrong-minded way of looking at the world. Being conflicted we live in fear.

- No one wants to share in conflict.
- No one in their *right mind* wants to be conflicted.
- No one in their *right mind* wants to offer conflict.

A conflicted teacher is a poor teacher and a poor learner, and the transfer value of a conflicted teacher is limited (T-7.VIII. 3:4&5).

2. Whatever we give away comes back. All projections boomerang. They come back immediately. The ego believes that we can get rid of something we do not want by throwing it away or projecting it outward. Giving, however, is how we keep something. Giving our judgments, we not only keep them, we reinforce them. Notice how often in conversation our talk consists of confirming prejudices. We project and then we become afraid that our projections will return to haunt us. If we say that someone is unworthy of God's love, we must believe that we are ourselves unworthy. Since projections never leave the minds, they still bother us. It's what we call guilt. We cannot perpetuate an illusion about others without perpetuating illusions about ourselves (T-7. VIII. 4:1). To get rid of guilt we need to forgive—to let go—to let the past be the past and the present the present.

> The game of life is the game of boomerangs.
> Our thoughts, deeds and words return to us
> sooner or later, with astounding accuracy.
> Florence Scovel Shinn

Whenever we are happy we are also giving, and love spontaneously pours forth from the heart. The principle of *generosity,* being one of those laws of cause and effect, works on the ego level and the spiritual level.

Whatever we give we receive.

If we project guilt—we receive guilt.
If we extend love—we receive love.
Whatever we give we get. Even more than we give do we receive.
This is the way guilt grows. This is the way love grows.

Sacrifice and Abundance

Traditional Christianity says it is necessary to sacrifice (*pay for*) or atone for our sins. Giving to the ego is sacrifice, but sacrifice is not giving. If we give because we feel we *have to* give, we are not giving. Giving *grudgingly* is not giving. The ego is subtle and will *give in order to get*. On an ego level we might try to put someone else in our debt as in: "Now you owe me." This is not giving. When we associate giving with sacrifice, we give because we believe that we will get something better, and can therefore do without whatever it is we give away.

> Giving to get is an inescapable law of the ego,
> which always evaluates itself in relation to other egos.
> T-4. II. 6:5

Spirit never loses since the more we give, the more we receive. We are all always giving and always receiving. We are always projecting or extending something. We are always giving our thoughts away. The gift of life is ours to give, because it was given to us. We are, however, unaware of our gift because we do not give it. If we do not extend the gift we both have, and are, we do not know our own being (T- 7. VII. 5:1-4).

We can give the light the world cannot give because it has been given to us. Because it was given to us, it is ours to give. As we give our light it shines—it glows. I'll bet that Jesus glowed—I'll bet he radiated incredible simplicity and wealth. We are being drawn by the light of God.

Feeling Called

> "Many are called but few are chosen."
> should be, "All are called but few choose to listen."
> Therefore, they do not choose right. The *chosen ones*
> are merely those who choose right sooner.

114

Right minds can do this now and they will find rest unto their souls. God knows you only in peace and this *is* your reality.

T- 3. IV.11:12-16

I went into the ministry as a young man because I wanted to search for God. The search for God is the ultimate business we are all about, just as it was for Jesus at the age of twelve when he said to his parents, "Don't you understand I have to be about my father's business?" Our business is to let our light shine. It's fun business. It's good business. It's the Holy Spirit's business. The more we let this light shine, the more it calls us from the world.

To lay the world aside means to understand the valuelessness of the world. The Kingdom of God is not of this world. That does not mean that we are to deny this world nor are we to refrain from living according to its laws. While in Rome, we must with some necessity live as the Romans do, without making a big deal of it. We can move ever deeper into letting this moment be as rich as it can be. The more we become aware of our Father's home, the more aware we become of the love that fills our hearts and pours into our minds.

Light is unlimited. It is abundant. If you have ever stood in the sun while it is warming your body and thought about the fact that it is warming half of the rest of the world, in exactly the same way in the same moment, then imagine the love of God, as reflected by the Holy Spirit, pouring forth into the minds of all who would receive it. The problem is not whether or not the light is there but whether or not we are blocking the light or are receptive to it.

One day I went to call on Amy Clark, an older lady who is now deceased, who was going into the hospital the next day to have an operation. While I was there, she received a call. Someone was offering her a ride to the hospital. She said that the previous day two other people had made the same offer. This is a perfect example of abundance. She had more than enough help. Several people had called and offered to help her with things she needed done. They did so because she was a lovely lady and people responded to her in love. She had no need to worry about worldly logistics like transportation.

On another occasion, Dolores and I met a remarkable lady at a check-out counter at Walmart. She was bright and cheery, with a hello and a positive comment about every item we were buying. I had noticed her doing the same thing to the customer before us. She did it with the one behind us. She gave positive affirmation to our good taste in having chosen such wonderful treasures. She was not just a good salesperson for the store, she was virtually lighting up the place. I made a comment about her cheery nature and a supervisor who was standing nearby turned and said that a customer had recently *written her up* for being such a plus for the store. The clerk told us that she loved retail and had been doing the same thing for 36 years. Her job is not glamorous and she probably earns little, but she has an excess of love to share with everyone and everyone she meets is richer for it.

> Today I learn the law of love;
> that what I give my brother is my gift to me.
> W-p II. Lesson 344

Acknowledging the Good—The Principle of Jen

Our task is not to *just* do good but to also acknowledge the good as it exists in our brothers and sisters. The Confucians believed in the principle of *Jen*—that at heart everyone is fundamentally good. Everyone at heart, as Spirit, as the true Self that they really are, is good. We cannot help being so when we are truly ourselves. It is when we are *not ourselves*, when we feel *out of sorts*, when the ego has a grip on us, that we find it difficult to give.

The movie *Regarding Henry* with Harrison Ford was about a tough-nut, unprincipled lawyer who gets shot in the head. He only slowly regains his memory and ability to work again, but when he comes back, it is as a changed man. He comes back innocent. He comes back having forgotten the training the world gave him. He is no longer cold, cruel and calculating. Deep inside each of us is a natural impulse to be good. This right-minded part of us has, however, been buried by the wrong-minded thought system of sin, guilt, fear and hatred. In order to remember who we really are we must look at this dark side of ourselves with the help of Jesus and then let it go in order to remember our innocence. Fortunately, we do not have to get shot in the head in order to remember our innocence.

116

Everyone has the same needs while they believe they inhabit a body:

- to share life with others.
- to be appreciated for the true Self that they are.
- to be able to work and be generative
  and productive and to have abundance to share.

As God's creative thought proceeds from Him to us, so must our creative thought proceed to our creations. We have the power to add to the Kingdom, and we claim this power as we become vigilant for God's Kingdom. When we are loving and giving, the creative power of God works through us.

When we are in love, we have an *automatic awareness* of the other's needs and we find it easy to be generous. The more we give our love away, the better things get, the more the other loves us, the more we love them, the greater our capacity for love. Marriages fail when one or both partners stop giving—stop nurturing—stop *extending.* If each partner gave 100% to the relationship there would be abundance—more than enough of what's needed.

Giving Our Forgiveness

There is nothing the world needs more than our forgiveness. Redemption is given to us to give each other. It is by giving redemption that we receive it. Only as we forgive do we have any idea what forgiveness is for ourselves. Forgiveness, like any form of giving, is reciprocal. Whenever we freely give (without letting the left hand know what the right hand is doing) we receive in ways immeasurable in ordinary terms.

To know light is to be light. It is to be present right here, right now. The more we give love, the more real love's presence becomes in our mind, thereby creating more love in our lives.

117

Chapter 12

The Law of Patience

Some say that my teaching is nonsense.
Others call it lofty but impractical.
But to those who have looked inside themselves,
this nonsense make perfect sense.
And to those who put it into practice,
this loftiness has roots that go deep.

I have just three things to teach:
simplicity, patience, compassion.
These three are your greatest treasures.
Simplicity in action and thoughts,
you return to the source of being.
Patient with both friends and enemies,
you accord with the way things are.
Compassionate toward yourself,
you reconcile with all beings in the world.
Lao Tzu

The eighth characteristic of a teacher of God is patience. Like all the other characteristics, patience rests on trust in a certain outcome. In patience we recognize that what is true is true.

I was talking on the phone with a friend and asked "What have you been doing?" She said, "Nothing," and I asked if she had been doing nothing well. There is an art to doing nothing well, to being in a quiet, receptive mind.

- The ego mind can't stop thinking
- worrying
- manipulating
- mixing everything up.

stip

One of the cardinal rules in writing a soap opera is that nobody gets to be happy. Happy ever after does not work in a soap.

118

The ego manipulates constantly. To stop worrying would be the death of the ego, so we must keep worrying to stay alive. The ego must have problems otherwise there is no ego. The ego cannot just let things be; there must be problems. But there are no problems in eternity. God does not have a problem; to the ego everything is problematic.

> When peace comes at last to those who wrestle
> with temptation and fight against the giving in to sin;
> when the light comes at last into the mind given to contemplation;
> or when the goal is finally achieved by anyone,
> it always comes with just one happy realization:
> *I need do nothing.*
> T-18. VII. 5:7

Simplicity, Patience, Compassion

Only when the mind is quiet and relaxed can we know God. We'll never get anywhere doing anything. "Doing" has gotten us into trouble. What we need is a quiet mind. In order to accomplish anything we must stop, shut down completely, and listen.

When the world starts becoming too much for us we start dreaming about simplicity. One of the books we sell at the Interfaith Center is *How To Want What You Have*. Another is *Simple Abundance*. There are quite a number of books about simplicity. When the world becomes too much for us, it's not surprising that we long for simplicity.

I once knew a man who worked in a global shipping department at the World Trade Center. Each day he talked with people all over the world. He was dealing with millions of dollars in sales and he had lots of employees who worked for and with him. One day at a party when we were sitting on a couch talking, he told me about his dream. His dream was to be a librarian in a small town. "Ah, that," he said, "would be the ideal life." He would love to live someplace where he could walk to work. But later I started wondering, if he were a librarian in a small town, would he be dreaming of the World Trade Center?

The Holy Spirit,
seeing where you are but knowing you are elsewhere,
begins His lesson in simplicity with the fundamental teaching
that *truth is true*.
This is the hardest lesson you will ever learn,
and in the end the only one.
Simplicity is very difficult for twisted minds.
T- 14. II. 2:1-3

This is an interesting thought: *The hardest lesson we will ever learn is the lesson of simplicity.* Why is it so hard for us to learn that *truth is true,* that the obvious is obvious? This is the only time in the entire Course that the phrase "the hardest lesson you will ever learn" is used. The hardest lesson we will ever learn is that what was never true is not true now, and never will be.

The ego mind has a hard time just letting things be. Everything has to be figured out; there must be some *system* by which everything can be understood. There are thousands of philosophies, psychologies, and religious systems that have attempted to figure things out and provide an explanation for everything. Someone figured out that we have fifty thoughts per minute which is equal to about 60,000 thoughts per day. And still we never figure it out.

I came to New York in 1967 to do doctoral work in philosophy at The Graduate Faculty of the New School specializing in German Idealistic Philosophy. I spent eleven years studying the works of Kant, Liebniz and Hegel, among others. These philosophical giants spent a lifetime trying to figure everything out. Hegel had an elaborate system of dialectics. No matter how much we might try to 'figure it out,' relying on the cogitation of our limited minds, we are not going to do it.

I have said that the last step
in the reawakening of knowledge is taken by God.
This is true, but it is hard to explain in words
because words are symbols,
and nothing that is true need be explained.

However, the Holy Spirit has the task of translating the useless into
the useful, the meaningless into the meaningful,
and the temporary into the timeless.
T-7. I. 6:3-5

Once when I had been meditating for a long time, I suddenly
started laughing, and I laughed for a *very* long time. A friend who
witnessed all this laughing asked what I was laughing about but I
could not explain it. There were no words for it. For a moment I had
a look into the absurdity of the universe and I laughed. The Course
says we should laugh at our fears and replace them with simplicity
and peace.

In a state of timelessness things just are. Everything just is.
There is nothing to control or manipulate. As much as the ego might
try, there is no getting away from God and the ego knows it. It knows
it is doomed and in that lies its fear, and that fear is its life.

Patience

Those who are certain of the outcome
can afford to wait, and wait without anxiety.
M-4. VIII. 1:1

Having made time, the ego also makes itself a slave to time.
If there is no time, there is no reason to be in a hurry. Sarah's cat
Pockets will sit at the sliding glass door which goes out onto the
deck, waiting either to be let in or out. If I go open the door, he will
very likely continue to sit there without moving. I must then wait for
him. Not being a creature of time, he can afford to wait. Can I afford
to wait? Is what is happening with me more important than what is
happening with him?

On a drive in the country a city slicker noticed a farmer
lifting one of his pigs up to an apple tree and holding the pig there as
it ate one apple after another. The farmer repeated this with a second,
then a third pig. "Maybe I don't know what I'm talking about," said
the city slicker, "but if you just shook the tree so the apples fell to the
ground, wouldn't it save a lot of time?" "Time," said the farmer.
"What does time matter to a pig?"

121

Patience relates to trust. If we find ourselves impatient about something, we do not trust the outcome. If I am impatient then I am afraid that if things don't happen when I want them to happen, they will not happen correctly. To be impatient is to be a victim of time. Lacking patience, I believe my peace of mind depends upon something external.

We live in a world where it is frequently necessary to wait in line at the bank, the grocery store, the ATM, the movies, and so on. We accept this. We wait in our cars for accidents, crowded conditions and construction delays. There is a story about a man whose car had stalled in heavy traffic as the light turned green. All his efforts to start the engine failed, and a chorus of honking behind him made matters worse. He finally got out of his car and walked back to the first driver and said, "I'm sorry, but I can't seem to get my car started. If you'll go up there and give it a try, I'll stay here and blow your horn."

Someone once said that the secret of patience is doing something else in the meantime. Waiting in line is a good time to do something else. Waiting is a good time to meditate. It is a good time to practice patience. The moment I notice I am beginning to get impatient I can say, like the man in the V-8 commercial who says, Hey I could have had a V-8! Hey, I could practice patience now! This line isn't going to move for a while, and I would rather wait with peace of mind than a distressed mind. I do not have to be stressed now." Waiting in line is simple. You just observe. You observe your own serenity and your own calmness in light of what, to the ego, might be perceived as a threatening situation. If God's love is eternal, what difference does time make?

Being patient does not mean ignoring time, being lackadaisical, late for work, missing appointments or acting irresponsibly. Living within time, I obey the laws of time, just as I must obey the laws of physics or the laws of the society of which I am a part, giving to Caesar that which is Caesar's and unto God that which is God's. There is no stress or anxiety in patience. If the cat doesn't go out the door when I open it or my child takes a long time to get ready, it doesn't really matter; I may still put my foot behind my cat and gently push him out the door, or I may ask Sarah to hurry up. I do it without being upset. I do it without anger.

There isn't any hurry and there is great peace of mind which comes in just letting things be. We can let things be when we are certain of the outcome. Eventually, we are all going to wake up and return home again. When we let things be there is no fear.

Patience is natural to the teacher of God.
All he sees is certain outcome,
at a time perhaps unknown to him as yet, but not in doubt.
M- 4. VIII. 1:2

You already are home, if you can see it. To remember home is to be at home. The Holy Spirit is already real. To call upon the Holy Spirit is to return home. Being late for an appointment or missing a deadline has nothing to do with eternity. To be impatient is to devalue God. Impatience is not trusting in God. To do the Course is just to continue to do what we are doing in the world. We continue to go about our work, to raise kids, but we do it with peace and with patience. Teachers of God are recognizable because they smile more frequently, their forehead is serene, their eyes are quiet (W-p1. 155. 1:2-4).

The Past Held No Mistakes

The time will be as right as is the answer.
And this is true for everything that happens now or in the future.
The past as well held no mistakes.
M-4. VIII. 1:6

Letting something which seems to be either great or small take the peace of God away from us is a waste of time. The way we see things makes all the difference in the world—quite literally. The way we walk to Heaven is exactly the way we were suppose to come. The further we are along the path, the more we can look back and see it was the perfect way for us. At this point we get to laugh at the absurdity of it all.

Patience affirms the fact that the past held no mistakes. Past mistakes hold no meaning in the real world. For each of us the process of awakening is highly individualized. In that sense it is also perfect. In patience we understand that regardless of what is going on in the world, we always have a choice and we can always choose forgiveness instead of anger, God instead of the ego. When we forgive it does not matter what happened in the past. Without the grievances which hold time in place, the idea of impatience is extraneous.

> Patience is natural to those who trust.
> Sure of the ultimate interpretation of all things in time,
> no outcome already seen or yet to come can cause them fear.
> M-4. VIII. 1:9&10

Trust is the first and most basic characteristic of a teacher of God. If you have trust you can have patience. If you have patience there is no hurry. You are not going anyplace. You are just going to *be* here. The ultimate interpretation is that made by the Holy Spirit. Patience and acceptance are synonymous. Patience comes in knowing that we have not forgotten Heaven, we only temporarily put it out of our minds. When we are sure of the outcome there is nothing that can upset us.

Our Patience With Each Other

> Your patience with your brother
> is your patience with yourself.
> Is not a child of God worth patience?
> I have shown you infinite patience
> because my Will is that of our Father,
> from Whom I learned of infinite patience.
> His Voice was in me as It is in you,
> speaking for patience towards the Sonship. . . .
> T-5. VI. 11:4-7

God is infinitely patient with us. We may wander about doing all sorts of things other than our Father's Will, yet God does not scold us nor does He desert us. In the introduction to the Course it says that while this is a required course the time we take it in is voluntary.

- No matter how long it may take us to come around to paying attention to Him,
  - no matter how far we may wander away,
  - no matter how much we may block our ears,

the Voice of the Holy Spirit is always there gently calling us home again. If God has infinite patience with us, can we then not demonstrate some patience with our brothers? There is great metaphysical power in acceptance, patience, perseverance, and consistency that enables us to break through illusions.

Only infinite patience produces immediate effects.
This is the way in which time is exchanged for eternity.
Infinite patience calls upon infinite love,
and by producing results now it renders time unnecessary.
T-5.VI. 12:1

It is possible to wake up now. Not for a single second do we need to wait. To be impatient is to be in a hurry. Impatient people are attached to fear and to time. Patience is never in a hurry. If we live in the present then there is nothing to be in a hurry for. Patient people are already there. There is not someplace else to go. Patient people know that no matter where you go—*there you are.* What matters is where the mind is.

A woman came to me anxious to gain some spiritual perspective. She was in need of some direction, and a friend had told her about the Course. She was upset when I had no books to give her, but I told her a new shipment was coming in the next week and that I would get one to her—which I did. She came to our study group for four weeks and then quit. One day I bumped into her in the grocery store and asked her if she was still studying the Course. She said no, that the Course was too slow. She said she needed answers now. I told her the answer was available now but she didn't want to hear it. She was looking for *magic,* not *miracles,* and I had no magic to give her.

Disraeli held that the secret of accomplishment consisted in being master of your subject, such mastery being attainable only through continual application and study. Mastery of the Course comes with patient application and study. The complexities that bind us in knots took us a lifetime to develop; and letting go is often slow. Answers are available now but you have to be patient to experience the results.

To have success with the Course, as with most things in life, you have to *hang in there*. We have to be able to get quiet enough, long enough, to hear the Holy Spirit.

Compassion

Only the sane can look on stark insanity and raving madness
with pity and compassion, but not with fear.
T- 19. IV(D).11:2

Our opening quote suggests we need to be compassionate with ourselves. The Course reminds us that when we meet anyone it is a holy encounter. As we treat our brothers and sisters so will we treat ourselves. As we think about others so will we think about ourselves (T-8. III. 4:1-3). Compassion is a matter of fellow feeling. It is a wonderfully blessed thing to feel with others, and to be moved to help and to offer our help whether the others ever know about it or not.

Face your deficiencies and acknowledge them;
but do not let them master you.
Let them teach you patience, sweetness, insight.
Helen Keller

I have just three things to teach:
simplicity, patience, compassion.
These three are your greatest treasures.
Lao Tzu

Chapter 13

The Law of Faithfulness

Faith is the force of life.
Tolstoy

There is no problem in any situation
that faith will not solve.
T-17. VII. 2:1

The Epileptic Boy
As they were rejoining the crowd, a man came up to him
and went down on his knees before him.
"Lord," he said, "take pity on my son:
he is a lunatic and in a wretched state;
he is always falling into the fire or into the water.
I took him to your disciples
and they were unable to cure him."
Jesus said in reply, "Bring him here to me."
And when Jesus rebuked it, the devil came out of the boy,
who was cured from that moment.
Then the disciples came privately to Jesus.
"Why were we unable to cast it out?" they asked.
"Because you have little faith.
I tell you solemnly,
if your faith were the size of a mustard seed
you could say to this mountain,
Move from here to there, and it would move;
nothing would be impossible for you."
Matthew 17: 14-20

The ninth characteristic of a teacher of God is faithfulness.

In Jesus' day, illnesses such as epilepsy and hysteria were
thought to be the work of the devil. What other possible explanation
could there be? People who were otherwise normal would suddenly

127

change and do things contrary to their ordinary behavior. It had to be explained somehow, and it was easy to blame an external source. The father in this story is particularly concerned about his son, for the boy would often hurt himself, falling into a fire or into water. The disciples tried to effect a cure but were unsuccessful and wondered about their failure. When we fail in anything it is not unusual for us to wonder why. Jesus tells the disciples that they failed because they lacked faith.

What Is Faith?

What is this thing that the disciples lacked? The Course speaks specifically about faith 400 times. To be faithful means to be consistent. We can always depend on a faithful friend. Faithfulness includes all the other characteristics of a teacher of God.

Being consistent, it is wholly honest.
Being unswerving, it is full of trust.
Being based on fearlessness, it is gentle.
Being certain, it is joyous.
And being confident, it is tolerant.
Defenselessness attends it naturally, and joy is its condition.
M-4. IX. 2:2-6 & 11

The goal of truth requires faith.
Faith is implicit in the acceptance of the Holy Spirit's purpose,
and this faith is all-inclusive.
Where the goal of truth is set, there faith must be.
T-17. VI. 6:1-3

Faith is:
• a secure trust in God and an acceptance of His Will.
• a confident belief in the truth.
• the expression of where we choose to place our trust.

We can place our faith in the ego and its ability to control and manipulate its way through the world, or we can have faith in the Holy Spirit. If we place our faith in the ego we find trouble. Placing our faith in the Holy Spirit gives us an optimistic outlook on life. It is then that we can look to what is holy in our brothers.

Rose Kennedy, the mother of John, Robert, Ted and six other children, suffered greatly with much loss in her life. When asked in an interview how she kept going in light of such tragedy she said it was her faith. She was talking about her faith as a Catholic, but it does not matter what one's religious background is. At Interfaith we appreciate all backgrounds and traditions. I've heard Ken Wapnick say on more than one occasion that while Mother Theresa sees Jesus very differently from the Course, it is only the theology that is different. A universal theology is impossible. What matters is that one have faith, as she did in the power of God.

Holiness cannot be seen except through faith (T-17. VIII. 4:3). If we have faith, then regardless how seemingly devastating, desecrating, or despoiling any situation might be, that faith can carry us through. That is why people with great faith find their way through life's toughest assignments. With faith we can face the loss of loved ones, illness and even our own death without despair and despondency.

A Rational Vision

A scientist arrives at a new discovery by making experiment after experiment after experiment, gathering fact after fact. Before he begins he must have some *vision* of what he expects to find. We do not come to important conclusions by chasing illusions. The process of making anything starts with what psychologist Erich Fromm called a *rational vision.* The history of science is full of examples of people who held to a rational vision or had what might be called *realistic optimism.* You could say that they placed faith in an outcome that was a rational vision of the truth of physics, even though they had little or no concrete proof. Bruno, Copernicus, Kepler, and Galileo all held to a vision of the sun and not the earth as the center of our solar system, even though the church burned Bruno at the stake, refused to allow Copernicus' works to be published and forced Galileo to recant his teaching.

Saying *it* the way *it* really is helps to make *it* real. The way *it* really is, is the way *it is* in God's Kingdom. As we see things in accordance with God's Will, we help to make God's Will manifest in our own lives.

I am a man of faith. My reliance is solely on God.

Mohandas Gandhi

In What Do We Place Our Faith?

Faith and desire go hand in hand
for everyone believes in what he wants.

T-21. II. 8:6

Each of us places our faith in something. If we see the world as fearful and threatening, then we may place our faith in lawyers, insurance policies, copyrights, patents, money, money markets, stocks and bonds, doctors, guard dogs, surveillance cameras, guns and nuclear arms and other forms of security. I'm not saying we should not have insurance. If having insurance makes you feel more peaceful then take out insurance. These things, however, are not lasting forms of security. There is a much deeper place any of us might place our faith—namely, in the reality of God's Kingdom.

Faithlessness

Faithlessness is not a lack of faith, but faith in nothing.

T- 21. III. 5:2

If we place faith in the ego we place our faith in nothing. The greatest faithlessness we can have is to affirm the reality of the ego and deny the reality of God.

- Faithlessness is the servant of illusion (T-17. VIII. 5:5).
- Faithlessness is sickness. It is sadness. It is pain.
- Faithlessness is seeing a brother as a body only.
- Faithlessness is a lack of vision.
- Faithlessness is depressing.
  Depression is the opposite of being inspired.

Faith is implicit in the acceptance of the Holy Spirit's purpose.

T- 17. VI. 6:2

130

There is no problem in any situation that faith will not solve (T-17. VII. 2:1). There is no problem so big that faith cannot see us through. The size of the problem matters not at all.

A lack of faith is the perception of the mind as impotent, but the right-mind is far from impotent. The Holy Spirit is far from impotent. The fact that miracles do not occur is an unnatural thing, not natural. Natural things are a part of God's Kingdom. It is natural to be happy. It is natural to assume that things are going to work out for the best.

> There is no cause for faithlessness,
> but there *is* Cause for Faith.
> T-17. VII. 8:7

If there is a problem that we need to solve and we haven't, it is because we placed our faith in our ego rather than in God. The Holy Spirit wants nothing other than what is absolutely best for us. Failure, or what we interpret as failure, comes from a lack of faith. At the end of each of his healings Jesus says: *Your faith has made you whole.* It is faith, wondrous faith, that makes miracles possible. How we live is determined by where we place our faith. Faith is trust in the guidance of the Holy Spirit despite difficulty, pain, persecution and confusion. With faith we don't have to try to manipulate the world to our way of seeing. Faith in God is the best insurance. In faith we see that the best is going to prevail despite obstacles.

> Faith is the opposite of fear
> as much a part of love as fear is of attack.
> T- 19.I. 10:1

Fostering Faith

We are called upon to place our faith in others and to trust that they, too, will be able to find their way through the maze of the ego till they are home once again. Faithlessness arises if we think our brother has done something against us. Yet, what we really blame him for is not what he did to us but what we did to him (T-17. VII. 8:2). We failed to offer him our forgiveness. It is not our brother's past we hold against him. It is our own agenda that gets in the way.

Our lack of faith in our brother arises because of our lack of faith in ourselves.

During the 1970s I had the opportunity to work with a wise teacher named Dr. Salvador Roquet. Salvador was a Mexican psychiatrist who gained his wisdom from studying Western medicine and from working with the native Indians of Mexico. On two different occasions I ventured to Mexico to work with him; on two other occasions he came to the States to work with a group of active seekers. At one point I went to Salvador to talk about a problem that I had not as yet overcome, to which Salvador confidently and simply replied "You will." I was struck by his faith in me, and I wanted very much to believe him. I was later able to set that problem aside in part because of Salvador's faith in me. Whenever I was a bit down or disheartened, Dr. Helen Schucman also fostered and encouraged my faith, assuring me that on a deeper level I knew what to do and she was sure I would make the right decision.

It's funny how faith in oneself works. The more we can place our faith and trust in God and go forward in faith, the more we find it growing inside. Mahatma Gandhi once said, "Faith is not something to grasp; it is a state to grow into." Just as Salvador and Helen placed their faith in me, so do I understand it is my pleasant task to foster faith in those who come to me for help. God has complete faith in us. As we trust in Him and place our faith in Him, we are healed and led home once again.

Forgiveness and Faith

Forgiveness is a precursor to miracles. The epileptic boy was thought to be possessed by a demon. He must have heard other people saying he was possessed. Having heard it, he must have believed it himself. He did have those fits where he would fall down and seem to be possessed. No one could heal him until someone looked at him with love. Even the disciples were unable to see the boy as whole. They must have been afraid of him, and they must have questioned their own ability to effect a cure. Once someone could look at the boy and see no evil in him, he could see himself as whole and be set free. We are ourselves set free as we look upon our brothers as whole. As the Course expresses it: "There is nothing faith cannot forgive" (T-19. I. 14:4).

Faith and forgiveness walk hand in hand. In faith there is no fear, no need to hold on to the unessential. Faith is a tool for the hero on the journey. It is the key to the Kingdom, the password that grants entrance to eternal life. The more willing we are to rest in faith and receive the guidance of the Holy Spirit, the more our vision is transformed and the more we experience the peace of God.

All-Inclusive Faith

Faith has need of the whole truth.
Pierre Teilhard de Chardin

The goal of truth requires all-inclusive faith. We cannot be fully committed sometimes. Faith is total commitment. As we give ourselves over to God and do His Will, peace comes progressively into our minds. If we do not believe we shall achieve what we wish to achieve—nothing is possible. With faith comes confidence. We must, however, have all-inclusive faith. We must trust totally.

The drought of the past winter threatened the crop in a village of Crete. The priest told his flock: "There isn't anything that will save us, except a special litany for rain. Go to your homes, fast during the week, believe and come on Sunday for the litany of rain." The villagers obeyed their priest, fasted during the week and came to church on Sunday morning, but as soon as the priest saw them, he was furious. He said: "Go away, I will not do the litany. You do not believe." "But Father," they protested, "we fasted and we believe." "If you believe," said the priest, "then where are your umbrellas?" This story makes a point about faith making our world better. Its metaphysical meaning shows us how committed we need to be to demonstrate our faith in the Holy Spirit's Atonement plan.

The mind can serve either ego or spirit, but it is only from the realm of spirit that we can really create. To be lacking in faith is to be heavy. To be lacking in faith is to believe in chains. Yet, we cannot help being free because we are spirit. Abundance in love and happiness comes from having faith. Abundance comes in understanding that things can only get better. Those who have faith abandon the belief in deprivation in favor of the abundance that belongs to them (T-1.IV.4:8). Faith is *rational vision*. It is *realistic optimism.* It is seeing the good. It is expecting the good. It is experiencing the good.

> What is dedicated to truth as its only goal
> is brought to truth *by* faith.
> T-19. I. 1:3

Faithlessness is dedicated to illusion but faith is dedicated to truth. Faith carries us past illusion.

The Calming of the Storm
One day he got into a boat with his disciples
and said to them,
"Let us cross over to the other side of the lake."
So they put to sea, and as they sailed he fell asleep.
When a squall came down on the lake,
the boat started taking in water
and they found themselves in danger.
So they went to rouse him saying,
"Master! Master! we are going down!"
Then he woke up and rebuked the wind and the rough water,
and they subsided and it was calm again.
He said to them, "Where is your faith?"
Luke 8: 22-25

Where Is Your Faith?
Jesus' disciples had many examples of his power and divinity before them. It is a wonder they could not have had more faith. In Peter's walking on the water, the story is the same. The moment he begins to doubt he begins to sink. Immediately Jesus says: "Where is your faith?" The disciples were perpetual witnesses to Jesus' miraculous power. They experienced directly the efficacy of his words. Yet they were lacking in faith.

Can we *let go* and trust the guidance of the Holy Spirit? Can we trust the power of our own right mind? Or, shall we choose to believe that we will never be whole? If Jesus tells us we can do even greater works than he, why don't we? If we wanted to—in love—we could overcome the obstacles to peace that linger and languish in our own heart. The good news of the Course is this: *that we can be set free.*

We are all free, all Sons and Daughters of God, all capable of the expression and experience of the reflection of the Kingdom of Heaven. Faithlessness is trusting in the ego and the ego is nothing, so placing our faith in the ego is placing our faith in nothing. It is an illusion which will one day fade and disappear completely. God is the all. He is everything. As we place our faith in Him, we discover everything—richness beyond measure, abundance, and eternal life.

Chapter 14

The Law Of
Open-Mindedness

The centrality of open-mindedness,
perhaps the last of the attributes the teacher of God acquires,
is easily understood when its relation to forgiveness is recognized.
M-X. 1:1

The tenth and final characteristic of a teacher of God is open-mindedness. There are thousands of different *forms* by which we might reach God; and there is no need to be judgmental about which form is better than another. Open-mindedness is central to the ancient Eastern religions of Hinduism, Buddhism and Taoism. There are literally thousands of different paths within the Hindu tradition. Hindus are sympathetic to a wide variety of different approaches to spirituality. Buddhism and Taoism also speak of an open mind in terms of the clarity, lucidity, and unclutteredness that is needed for true perception.

When we are open-minded our minds are not closed to anything or anyone. We have no investment in how this world is supposed to work—no predetermined, expected, or required outcome. If *"All things are lessons God would have me learn"* (Lesson 193), then *all* things are lessons God would have me learn *without exception*. The Law of Open-Mindedness thus means that my mind is not closed to any forgiveness lesson that comes my way. This chapter begins by saying that open-mindedness is *central* in the mind of Christ.

Picture open-mindedness as a vast space. Picture yourself in the center of this vastness. You are just one point—one little point of centrality. Clarity is possible when there are no blocks to the awareness of love's presence, no clouds preventing true perception.

136

When we are open-minded there are no complexes, no hang-ups, no knots within our psychic system.

Judgment Closes the Mind

Open-mindedness is *perhaps the last of the attributes a teacher of God acquires.* Why the last? Why not the first, if open-mindedness is so central to the discovery of our identity? Perhaps we must first develop trust, honesty, tolerance, patience, and the other attributes before our mind can be completely open. In fact, as we read: "Open-mindedness comes with lack of judgment. As judgment shuts the mind against God's Teacher, so open-mindedness invites Him to come in" (M-X. 1:2&3). Tolerance, or the lack of judgment, is the third characteristic of a teacher of God. Tolerance comes before open-mindedness because judgment closes the mind. The first judgment, the first tiny, mad idea, is that I sinned. I did something against God and now I am afraid of God. This world is the result of our attempts to get away from God. What keeps me from God is my judgment that leads to separation. It is also the judgment I continue to make in each and every instant.

> As condemnation judges the Son of God as evil,
> so open-mindedness permits him to be judged
> by the Voice for God on His behalf.
> M-X. 1:4

The Voice for God is the Holy Spirit. Only the Holy Spirit can judge truly.

Marlo Morgan in her book, *Mutant Message Downunder,* tells the tale of spending several months on a walkabout with an Aboriginal tribe in Australia. There is a chapter entitled "Cordless Phone" in which she tells a delightful story. One day, a young man of the tribe asked the elders if he could run ahead, and they gave him permission. Later in the day the tribe stopped dead in their tracks. When Morgan asked what was going on she was told that the young man who had run ahead had killed a kangaroo and was calling back (telepathically) to ask if he could cut off the tail in order to lighten his load. He was given permission and the tribe began to dig a pit and build a fire to cook the kangaroo. A couple of hours later the young man came walking into camp carrying dinner for the tribe.

When she asked how they could talk telepathically, Morgan was told that it was possible because they had *open minds*. They did not have any secrets from each other. I used to make retreats at a Trappist Monastery, New Mellery Abbey near Dubuque, Iowa. There, I noticed that the monks had developed an ability to talk to each other telepathically. I was watching two of them working on a stone wall. There was a bird singing prettily in a nearby tree and one of them stopped to look up at the bird. Then the other one also looked up. Then they looked at each other as though to say, "How nice." Then they began their work again. There were many similar instance of this clear nonverbal communication.

What we keep hidden closes the mind. The more we keep hidden, the more we close things off and the more terrified we become of the world, and of God. If I have nothing to hide it doesn't matter if someone else looks at my thoughts. According to the Aborigines, Westerners cannot read each other's minds because they have a great deal to hide. We are very well-defended. Our defenses keep us from knowing each other. Our defenses keep us from knowing God. We believe we can have thoughts we would not share with another. Salvation for the ego consists in keeping these thoughts to ourselves alone. The more we hide the less open we are to full communication with others and with God (T- 15. IV. 7:2-5).

According to the Aborigines with whom Morgan lived, mental telepathy is the way humans were designed to communicate. Different languages and written alphabets are eliminated as obstacles as we become more sensitive to the thoughts and feelings of other people. It's hard to be sensitive when we have lots of defensive blocks built up around us. Sensitivity to inner guidance requires open-mindedness. When we engage in deception, fraud and subterfuge, we hide our thoughts and feelings and block others' perception. Once there is nothing to hide, once there is no blockage, it is easier to be receptive to inner guidance.

Watch carefully and see what it is you are really asking for.
Be very honest with yourself in this,
for we must hide nothing from each other.
T-4.III. 8:1

According to Marlo Morgan, Aboriginal people don't think the voice was designed for talking. Real talking is done with the heart and for that we don't need vocal cords. The voice, they feel, was made for singing, for celebrating and healing.

> *Later during our journey when they worked with me to develop my mental communication, I learned, as long as I had anything in my heart or my head I still felt necessary to hide, it would not work. I had to come to peace with everything, to lay my mind out on a table like the Real People do, and stand by as my motives were exposed and examined. I had to learn to forgive myself, not to judge but to learn from the past. They showed me how vital it was to accept, be truthful and love myself so I could do the same with others.*
> Marlo Morgan, *Mutant Message Downunder*, MM CO, 1991, p. 65

Adam bit into the fruit of the knowledge of good and evil, and when he did, his mind was divided. A divided mind is not a clear mind. It is caught between *yes* and *no*, *back* and *forth*, *maybe* and *maybe not*. When we allow the Holy Spirit to judge for us, and there is no split mind, nothing is evil.

> A separated or divided mind *must* be confused.
> It is necessarily uncertain about what it is.
> It has to be in conflict because it is out of accord with itself.
> T-3. IV. 3:4-6

Open-mindedness is the opposite of close-mindedness. When we are angry we shut ourselves off from others. We might cross our arms, we close our fists. Close-mindedness is defensive. Open-mindedness is a freeing experience just as closing the mind locks one within oneself. Open-mindedness allows the Holy Spirit to work through us.

> As the projection of guilt upon him would send him to hell,
> open-mindedness lets Christ's image be extended to him.
> Only the open-minded can be at peace,
> for they alone see reason for it.
> M-X. 1:5&6

The open mind accepts everything. Accepting everything, we love everything. If I project my guilt onto you and damn you to hell, I condemn myself. When I let go of my judgments, the image of Christ can come through.

Forgiveness or Undoing

How do the open-minded forgive?
They have let go all things that would prevent forgiveness.
M-X. 2:1

Forgiveness does not *do* anything! It *undoes*. It clears away the mess. It opens the mind. It removes interferences to an awareness of love's presence. Our task is not to seek for love, but to seek out all the barriers we built against love. It is not necessary to seek for what is true. It is necessary, however, to recognize what is false in order to let go of it (T-16. IV. 5:9-11).

We do not have to figure out what is true. We cannot. All we have to do is join with the Holy Spirit in our right mind and allow His love to undo through forgiveness. We actually know a lot more about what is false than we know about what is true. We have been living with the false for a long time. The false is whatever we feel guilty about. The false is whatever is bothering us. It is the thing we are afraid to talk about. Removing the interference through forgiveness is all that is needed. Going ahead and changing our minds we will speak the truth. Once that is done, the love that is already there will come to the fore. Our judging, our evaluating, our blaming and accusing, our attacking, our aggression and our guilt all keep us from seeing. We let them go as we recognize that we do not need them and do not want them.

The Open-minded have in truth abandoned the world,
and let it be restored to them in newness and in joy so glorious
they could never have conceived of such a change.
M-X. 2:3

Becoming a teacher of God is a very worthwhile occupation. It's the only occupation that makes us feel completely whole. To renounce the world simply means that there is nothing of this world that holds sway over us. It does not mean going off and living in a cave. Neither does it mean *not* going off and living in a cave. It simply means looking at this world through eyes of love rather than condemnation. Seeing the real world involves a change in the way we look upon the world. When the world of sin, guilt, sickness and sorrow disappears, we are inevitably left with peace.

Nothing is now as it was formerly.
Nothing but sparkles now
which seemed so dull and lifeless before.
And above all are all things welcoming, for threat is gone.
M-X. 2:4-6

I have a friend, Tom Baker, who used to be a priest. Tom spent some time in a Trappist monastery where silence is observed and a great deal of time is spent in praying and chanting. One morning he was walking down a path on the monastery grounds, just looking at the path, when all of a sudden he noticed that the grass was full of light. He looked up and the trees were also full of light. He looked over and saw the barn was also full of light. In that moment, he said, everything communicated to him; what they said was, "We're happy!" Everything sparkled and told him that: "We're happy!" just being grass and trees and a barn. In perfect innocence there is nothing to be afraid of and there is much to be happy about.

Just Let It Go!

With an open mind all things are welcomed because all things are seen as lessons in the life journey. Even that which may seem *terrible* as the world defines it has its place. As we realize that what seems to be fearful and horrible is nothing, it becomes possible to let it go. When friends bring me a problem on which they feel really stuck I often say, "Let it go." It may be the last thing they want to hear because their mind is *stuck* on the problem, but so often it is exactly the right answer. Given some time, they can usually see that the best solution is just to let it go!

Jesus was betrayed, beaten, abandoned and crucified. Yet, he never saw himself as persecuted, never got upset or angry with the disciples who left him. Believing that something can hurt me does not make it true. So often with Sarah, the thing around which I could

141

get angry *is really nothing,* and the simplest solution is to let it go. It is so much more healing. "Letting it go" is a law of open-mindedness. The moment the place of *stuckness* is recognized: "Let it go. Let it go. Let it go."

No clouds remain to hide the face of Christ.
Now is the goal achieved.
M-X. 2:7&8

The face of Christ is a symbol of forgiveness. This does not mean that if we want to see the face of Christ we should squint our eyes and get up close to someone and try to focus on them. Forgiveness changes nothing in the world of form. The only change happens within one's mind. When we look at the world through the eyes of innocence, we simply cannot see sin, guilt and fear. Clouds are symbols of ego illusions that block our vision.

The final goal of the Course is not Heaven or God. The final goal is peace, and forgiveness is the means for attaining peace. The Course is a curriculum of undoing. A miracle *undoes.* Forgiveness undoes all the things the ego placed in our mind. What is left is the love of God that automatically comes to the fore once the blocks to the awareness of love's presence are removed.

Love is not learned but remembered. What we can learn is how to allow the Holy Spirit to undo the whole ego thought system of attack, sickness and death. We need a thought system that is going to teach us how to undo. Once we undo everything that would hurt and harm us, our minds are open. Open-mindedness is the last characteristic of a teacher of God. There is now nothing left to clutter the mind—no animosity, no attack thoughts, no feeling sorry for oneself, nothing. The formula of the Course is
that we see the face of Christ in our brother,
thereby remembering God's love.

Our Natural Inheritance
The characteristics of a teacher of God are not the characteristics of Heaven. They are reflections of how one can live in the world without the ego's thought system. When the Holy Spirit has completely undone the ego's thought system, what is left are the

reflections of Christ in this world. The list of attributes of God's teachers does not include things that are the Son of God's inheritance. Terms like love, sinlessness, perfection, knowledge and eternal truth do not appear in the list of attributes of a teacher of God (M-X. 3:1-3). We do not have to seek for love, for sinlessness, perfection, knowledge and eternal truth. They have always been our natural inheritance and are restored to us once we sweep away the clouds of guilt that kept us from seeing.

> It is the function of God's teachers
> to bring true learning to the world.
> Properly speaking it is unlearning that they bring,
> for that is true learning in the world.
> M-X. 3:6&7

True Perception Meditation
There is nothing you need to think about.
Nothing.
Your mind is completely open.
There is nothing that possesses it.
There are no judgments to make.
There is no reason to be upset or worried
about anything.
Accept everything just the way that it is.
When your mind is completely open it will also be
certain, clear, and sure.
Then nothing can disturb your peace of mind.
Open-mindedness is a state of peace
because it is uncluttered.
Say: "There is no one against whom I hold any anger.
There is no one I would attack in any way."
When this is true, when the mind is completely open,
I am completely free!

It is easy to choose for the ego because we are always doing it. The ego is obvious. It is out there in the world. The ego knows how to *Go for it!* and *Get it!* We don't want to go inside. We don't want to meet God. God is scary. *If God wins I lose,* or so thinks the ego. We are afraid that if we turned everything over to God we would be destroyed. On an ego level this is true—the ego disappears in the face of God. What we are left with, however, is not nothing, but everything. Then and only then do we truly live, for only then can we be ourselves. The added benefit of an open mind is that when the mind is open and clear, we can actively work on fulfilling our destiny. Whatever we want to work on, we can work on easily and other people will help us.

Postscript:

Fulfilling My Function Is My Happiness

You are not at peace
because you are not fulfilling your function.
T- 4. I. 9:4

The Story of the Golden Buddha

In 1957 a group of monks in Thailand had to move a clay Buddha from their temple to a new location. The monastery was to be relocated to make room for the development of a highway through Bangkok. When the crane began to lift the giant Buddha, the weight was so tremendous that it cracked. Rain began to fall and the head monk, concerned about damage to the Buddha, decided to lower the statue to the ground and cover it with a tarp to protect it from the rain.

Later he went to check on the Buddha. Shining a flashlight under the tarp, he saw a little glitter shining back at him. Taking a closer look at the sparkle of light, he wondered if there was something under the clay. He got a chisel and hammer and began to chip away. As he knocked off pieces of clay, the gleam grew brighter and brighter. Many hours later the monk stood face to face with an extraordinary solid gold Buddha.

Historians believe that several hundred years before, when the Burmese army was about to invade Thailand, Siamese monks covered their beloved Golden Buddha with an outer layer of clay in order to keep their treasure from being looted by the Burmese. Unfortunately, the Burmese slaughtered all the Siamese monks, so the secret of the Golden Buddha remained intact until 1957. (This story was originally told to me by one of the parishioners of our church in New York City who had seen the Golden Buddha. I later read the account as told by Jack Canfield in *Chicken Soup for the Soul*, Vol. 1, Health Communications, Inc., 1993).

What's inside all of us is golden, not in our bodies but in the us that we truly are. Inside each of us there is the Christ, the Buddha, the Son of God waiting for an opportunity to manifest. Nothing could make us happier than to fulfill our function. Our function is to realize the love within ourselves, to complete the atonement, to be who we were meant to be. The ego would have us believe that our function is misery. It would have us believe that we are destined to wander about without ever becoming aware of our true identity. It is your destiny and my destiny to become a realized Son or Daughter of God. Nothing else will ever be fulfilling. Nothing else will ever completely satisfy. God gives us only happiness. *Love cannot give evil and what is not happiness is evil* (W-66. 6:3).

Plato and Buddha both said that it is possible to realize an ideal eternal state that has nothing to do with the little self of everyday life. Plato, Buddha and Jesus all said it is possible to know this Self as the true Sons of God that we really are. The ego made space and time. Having made space and time we got caught in space and time. Our egos believe that our life is limited, that we are liable to be sick, or rejected, or hurt, or even to die.

Is Perfection Possible?
When we study the lives of the saints, regardless of the religious tradition, we discover that they were men and women who were completely devoted to the search for God. When we read the details of their lives we discover that, like you and me, they too had many struggles to go through. St. Francis of Assisi strove constantly to keep God first in his life—yet St. Francis was also caught in the ego. He lost his temper and got angry, which suggested that he had not reached perfection. Yet, despite these shortcomings, his search for God was so intent that even his contemporaries thought of him as a saint.

Is it possible while we are here, living within the confines of a body, to reach a state of perfection? Ambrose Bierce has suggested that perfection is "an imaginary state." Emile Zola once said that the idea of striving for perfection is: ". . . such a nuisance that I often regret having cured myself of using tobacco." While caught in ego, perfection will always seem illusory. As children of God we are already perfect. Consequently, many spiritual traditions say that our task is not one of doing anything in the world. It is a matter of undoing or remembering who we already are. It is simply a matter of *waking up* or *coming back* to ourselves. While we are caught in a world of illusion, however, Heaven seems like a dream but Heaven is the only thing that is real. All else is an illusion. "Perfection *is* and cannot be denied" (T-12. II. 8:6).

Beginning the Search—Choosing Again

The first step in the search for perfection is to work on it. In a twelve step program like Alcoholics Anonymous, the first step is a recognition that, left to one's own devices, life has gotten out of hand; therefore it is better not to try to do things on one's own but to turn everything over to a higher power.

Jesus began his ministry in ancient Israel with the single word, *Repent* (Matthew 3:2). Repent means *to look at things differently*; to look at things another way; to choose once again. When we repent we recognize that we need help. After the word repent Jesus says, *for the Kingdom of God is at hand.* The real world is as close as our hand. It is right in front of us. We don't have to go anywhere to find it. All we have to do is *see* it. The Golden Buddha is inside every one of us.

The Kingdom of Heaven is here. It is now. And it is inside us. Not in our bodies but in the Mind that has always been connected to God. Its position is not going to change. We may believe that we cannot find Heaven, but Heaven can find us. Awareness of our true reality is something perfectly natural, not something we have to struggle for. Only the ego struggles. We don't need to struggle to reach something; we only need to let ourselves *be.* Perfection is being true to our own nature which is a reflection of the Oneness of God and Christ while we are in our bodies.

Host to God or Hostage to the Ego

We choose to be either hostage to the ego or host to God (T-11. II. 7:1). The ego *seems* to demand less of us than God so we

147

choose for the ego. On the whole we do not work on developing an inner life. Going to church, observing rituals, singing songs and listening to preachers doesn't mean we are leading a spiritual life unless something changes inside. If we continue to hold on to our individual prejudices and our righteous indignation nothing has changed. Sogyal Rinpoche, author of *The Tibetan Book of Living and Dying,* says that when he asked his master what it was about Western culture that was different from Eastern culture, the master responded that Westerners were great time wasters. The Course says we can temporize and we are capable of enormous procrastination (T-2. III. 3:3).

When we fulfill our function, we live in love rather than fear. We do what the Holy Spirit would have us do, which is what we really want to do; everything works to our greater happiness and we cannot help feeling good about the whole of life. The more we let ourselves be one with God—the more we discover our own true nature—the more we reach perfection.

Perfection is to be like God in unity of spirit.
William of St. Thierry

I watched a show about a boy who was paralyzed from birth with asphyxia, a condition in which there is insufficient oxygen in the body. His parents began to notice when he was quite young that, although he could not talk, he was obviously quite bright. Eventually, with the right kind of help, he was taught to read and write. They then discovered that he was, in fact, quite bright and could write beautiful poetry. His poetry was a simple yet profoundly clear description of the things he saw. He had a way of seeing that was keen and much sharper than most of us. His whole countenance seemed perfect—though he lived within the confines of a distorted body. His story and many others like it help confirm the non-reality of the body.

Life is Nothing Without God

There are times when, like this young man, we are brought close to God through difficult circumstances. Whenever life becomes too much for us—when we need help because we are sick or in debt, or our relationships are falling apart—we often turn to God. At such moments we recognize that there is no life apart from God. It does not matter how successful we have been in the world. Our lives may be rich, exciting, and beneficial to others, but if we can't remember who we are in truth, we gain nothing. Jesus in the Gospels asks us what benefit it would be for us "to gain the whole world and lose our own soul" (Mark 8:36 and Luke 9:25). In the Course He says that we cannot lose our soul, but we can lose our awareness of it (T-5. II. 7:12-14).

> Perfection alone gives meaning to life.
> Logan P. Smith

Everyone is on the road to perfection: the murderer, the minister and the mystic. We cannot know our own perfection until we honor everyone who was created like us. Everyone is struggling to get back home, to reach again to perfection. Jesus tells us repeatedly that our task is to remember that which gives us life in the first place. As He was to express it in the Gospels: "Life does not consist of bread alone but of every word that proceeds from the mouth of God" (Matthew 3:4). The important thing is the remembrance of God. We never really lost God, but only for a moment forgot Him. Never are we to abandon the search for God. God is our only hope. The alternative is despair.

Perfection Means Giving Up Projection

> Only my condemnation injures me.
> Only my own forgiveness sets me free.
> W-pI. 198. 9:3&4

To be aware of who we are in perfection we need to release all our projections. It requires living according to the laws of trust, honesty, tolerance, gentleness, joy, defenselessness, generosity, patience, faithfulness and open-mindedness. It is possible to put God first regardless of the circumstances of our lives. It is possible to fulfill our function of forgiveness and find our greatest happiness. Our happiness and our function are one because God has given us both.

What Else?

If you enjoyed this book you might enjoy

On Course Magazine:
Inspiration For The Inner Journey
On Course is published every other month
and costs $6.00 per issue for 3rd class or
$8.00 per issue for delivery by first-class
mail inside a protective envelope.

A subscription to **On Course**
can be ordered through:

The Interfaith Center
25 South Street, Washingtonville, NY 10992
800-275-4809

Please visit us at our 11 AM Sunday services in New York City.
Interfaith Fellowship
Cami Hall, 165 W. 57th St. (Across from Carnegie Hall)

Jon is available for lectures and workshops internationally
and can be reached at the above number.

- Additional Reading -

Berke, Diane. *Love Always Answers.* New York, Crossroads, 1994.
_____. *The Gentle Smile.* New York, Crossroads, 1995.

Coit, Lee. *Listening.* Available from Las Brisas Retreat Center,
PO Box 500, Wildomar, CA 92595-0500. Lee is also the author of
Accepting.

Hotchkiss, Burt. *Your Owner's Manual.* Fernwood Management,
25441 Rice Rd., Sweet Home, OR 97386-9620.

Dr. Jampolsky, Gerald, *Love Is Letting Go of Fear.* New York,
Bantam, 1984 (Attitudinal Healing, 19 Main St., Belvedere-Tiburon,
CA 94920-2507)
_____. *Teach Only Love: The Seven Principles of Attitudinal
Healing.* New York, Bantam, 1984.

Mundy, Jon. *Awaken To Your Own Call: Exploring A Course In Miracles.* New York, Crossroads, 1994.

_____. *Listening To Your Inner Guide.* Crossroads, New York, 1994.

Perry, Robert. *Introduction to "A Course in Miracles."* Available from Robert Perry, PO Box 4238, West Sedona, AZ 86340-4238. Robert is also the author of *The Elder Brother: Jesus in A Course in Miracles* and an ongoing series of booklets on the *Course.*

Raub, John Jacob. *Who Told You You Were Naked? Freedom from Judgment, Guilt, and Fear of Punishment.* New York, Crossroads, 1992.

Singh, Tara Singh. *A Course in Miracles: A Gift for All Mankind.* Los Angeles, Life Action Press, 1992. Tara Singh is also the author of many other books. (Foundation for Life Action, 902 S. Burnside Ave., Los Angeles, CA 90036).

Wapnick, Dr. Kenneth Wapnick. *A Talk Given On A Course in Miracles*, A good introduction to the Course. Available from Foundation for *A Course in Miracles*, RR 2, Box 71, Roscoe, NY 12776-9506

_____. *Absence from Felicity: The story of Helen Schucman and Her Scribing of "A Course in Miracles,"* 1991.

_____. *Forgiveness and Jesus: The Meeting Place of "A Course in Miracles."* Roscoe, NY, Foundation for *A Course in Miracles.* Addresses the misunderstandings of traditional Christianity and distinguishes these from the teachings of the Course.

Watson, Allen. *A Healed Mind Does Not Plan.* The Circle of Atonement. PO Box 4238. West Sedona, AZ 86336.

Williamson, Marianne. *Return to Love: Reflections on A Course in Miracles.* New York, Harper Collins, 1992. (Forty-two weeks on the bestseller list in 1992. Miracles Projects, 1550 N. Hayworth Ave., Los Angeles, CA 90046-3337)